My
Prayer
Book

Presented to _____

_____

By _____

_____

My Prayer Book

My Prayer Book

Concordia ®
Publishing House
St. Louis

Copyright 1957

Revised Edition, © 1980

CONCORDIA PUBLISHING HOUSE

Saint Louis, Missouri

Library of Congress Catalog Card No. 56-12420

ISBN 0-570-03012-9

MANUFACTURED IN THE UNITED STATES OF AMERICA

Preface

"The prayer of a righteous man has great power in its effects" is more than a striking sentence or a beautifully phrased paragraph. Faith in God, to whom we pray, is more important than the wording of the prayer. "Let him ask in faith, with no doubting, for he who doubts is like a wave of the sea that is driven and tossed by the wind. For that person must not suppose [he] . . . will receive anything from the Lord" (James 1:6-8). The wording of our prayer is of secondary importance. Indeed, Jesus once indicated that words are not even necessary for an acceptable prayer. "Your Father knows what you need before you ask Him" (Matthew 6:8).

Words, however, give expression to what is in our hearts. When, therefore, His disciples asked Jesus, "Lord, teach us to pray," the Master gave them the words of the model prayer, "The Lord's Prayer." Jesus Himself poured out His heart to His heavenly father in words of a long prayer in the night in which He began His suffering for our redemption (John 17).

In adding this revised MY PRAYER BOOK to the abundance of devotional and prayer books published in recent years, it is our hope not only to have provided acceptable, prepared prayers, but also to have offered suitable prayer patterns to aid those who find it difficult to express what is in their hearts as they face the problems and temptations, the joys and sorrows, the successes and disappointments of life.

"Let us then with confidence draw near to the Throne of grace, that we may receive mercy and find grace to help in time of need" (Hebrews 4:16).

CONCORDIA PUBLISHING HOUSE

Contents

Prayers for Christian Worship

Prayers for the Family Life

Prayers for Various Occupations

Morning and Evening Prayers

THE FIRST WEEK

Sunday Morning

Eternal and everlasting Father, in whose presence I pass my fleeting years, upheld by Your grace and power, make Your love real to me as I worship You today. Grant that Your Holy Spirit may strengthen my faith and my resolve to serve You with greater faithfulness. May nothing be more precious to me than the Gospel of the redeeming love of Your Son Jesus, my Savior.

Create in me a clean heart. Remove all distracting thoughts from my mind as I come into Your presence to hear Your Word and make my prayers and my confession of faith to You. May I deeply appreciate the great love of Your Son, who went to Calvary to pay for my many sins with His own lifeblood. Forgive me daily. May the suffering of my Savior and His pain on the cross open my eyes to the marvels of His love and the greatness of my sin. Fill my heart with peace and the joy of forgiveness.

Accomplish Your will in me. Strengthen my resolution to serve You more faithfully. Help me to overcome all sluggishness to worship You and all indifference to Your Word. Let me conquer my fears and my self-pitying moods. On this day of worship let me sing praises to You. Help me to dedicate myself again to Your Son Jesus Christ, who rose from the dead and lives forevermore. Amen.

Sunday Evening

As this day comes to a close, I gratefully acknowledge Your goodness and mercy, O Lord, in granting to me the privilege of hearing Your Word, the glorious Gospel of my salvation. Your promises enable me to look upward with confidence and forward with courage. Bless the labors of my hands. Help me understand my duties and tasks. Enrich my week with blessings from Your bountiful hands. Grant me the grace to live daily in Your presence, doing the things pleasing to You and helpful to my companions on the way.

Deepen my love for You. Keep me faithful to Your Word, and help me to follow the directives given me today. Forgive all my sins, especially every indifference of heart toward Your Gospel. Bless me this night, and protect all Your children. Bless my family, my friends, my pastor, and my church. Bless my co-workers throughout this week with Your gracious benedictions. In Jesus' name I ask this. Amen.

Monday Morning

Gracious God, heavenly Father, I thank You for Your mercy, which has kept me from all harm and danger through the darkness of the night. Erase the darkness of sin from my life by Your forgiveness, for Jesus my Savior's sake.

Let me begin my duties today with the assurance that You will look with favor on my work. Bless whatever I do that my wages may be enough for my needs and the wants of those whom You have committed to my care. Teach me to give cheerfully of my earnings to support Your church and to help the poor and needy. Help me to remember today the admonition of my Savior: "Seek first His kingdom and His righteousness, and all these things shall be yours as well." In that spirit let me begin my tasks. Amen.

Monday Evening

O God of love and grace, this evening I humbly ask You to forgive me for Jesus' sake all that was wrong in my life today.

I confess that at times I find myself doing what I do not want to do, and sometimes not doing what I know I should do. Have mercy on me! Send Your Holy Spirit to me that I may grow in grace and in the knowledge of Jesus Christ, my Savior. Help me be full of those things that are pleasing to you.

I thank You for the good health with which You have blessed me so that I can do the work I have been given. Remember all who are distressed by sickness and sorrow, and apply to their wounded hearts the healing balm of Your precious promises.

Let peaceful sleep close my eyes tonight, and if it be Your will, awaken me in the morning refreshed in body and soul. When my last night on this earth comes, let me see the more perfect day in glory everlasting. For Jesus' sake. Amen.

Tuesday Morning

Heavenly Father, let Your will be done on earth as it is in heaven. Grant that Your will may be done in the hearts and lives of people everywhere. Grant me the grace to always be aware of Your will and to submit to You in all things. Give me faithfulness in my work, and crown my labors with Your blessing.

Restrain the rulers of the earth who place their will above Yours and thereby cause suffering and heartache among their people. Help them see that peace and good order can prevail only as long as Your will is done.

Convince all ministers of the Gospel that Your will is done when they preach and teach Your Word in truth, when they admonish the erring and comfort the sorrowing, and when they point their hearers to Christ and You.

Keep me and all Christians mindful of Your commandments and of our duty to serve You. Above all, give us a burning love for souls and a sense of urgency in proclaiming the free salvation that You have made ours through Jesus Christ.

May I trust in Your promises and ask no more than You have promised. In prosperity keep me humble. In adversity keep me strong. At all times give me a deep devotion to duty and confident trust in Your mercy, through our Lord and Savior Jesus Christ. Amen.

Tuesday Evening

Dear Father in heaven, I thank You for Your care and protection, for the health and strength necessary for the work of today and for the answer to my prayers and the prayers of Christians everywhere.

Be with me tonight and keep all harm and danger from me. Forgive my sins, and assure me of Your abiding grace and mercy. Keep all who are near and dear to me in Your watchful care. Give me a quiet, restful sleep, and thereby prepare me for my work tomorrow.

Cleanse my heart from all thoughts of hate or envy, and help me to live peaceably with all people.

Make me helpful, kind, and considerate that I may live my life for You and for others.

May thoughts of You be in my heart when I fall asleep and when I awake. If this night should be my last on earth, may I fall asleep in Jesus and awake in Your presence. Amen.

Wednesday Morning

Lord Jesus, You are my everliving and everloving Savior, I thank You that You never sleep and that You have protected me by Your mighty hand through the night.

Open my eyes to see the blessings that You have prepared for me today. For the love of friends which will enrich this day, I thank You. For the ability to work and to serve others, I praise You. For the gifts to be granted me this day, I honor You.

Keep me firm in faith, watchful in temptation, humble in my successes, and joyful in the face of afflictions, for Your name's sake. Without You I can do nothing, but I can do all things through You, who strengthens me.

Help me today to bear clear witness to the hope begotten in me by Your resurrection from the dead. Grant me Your Holy Spirit that I may be dead to sin and alive to holiness. Use me today to bring Your Gospel to some persons who are like sheep without a shepherd, so that they may learn to know You, the

Good Shepherd, and find in You rest and peace for their souls.

Lead me in the paths of righteousness this day, Lord Jesus, for Your name's sake. Amen.

Wednesday Evening

At the end of another day, dear heavenly Father, I praise You for Your goodness and adore You for Your mercy. You did not leave me or forsaken me, even as You promised. But I have failed You and forsaken You by sinning, and I ask You, for the sake of Your Son and my Redeemer, to cleanse me from all my sins.

From the rising of the sun to the shadows of tonight You have been with me to bless, help, guide, strengthen, and comfort me. I am not worthy of the least of all the mercies and of all the truth which You have shown to me, Your servant. I thank You, Father.

I ask You to look with tender pity on all who are without the comfort of Your Gospel. Turn their hearts to repentance and to faith in Your Son, and cause Your Gospel of forgiveness to be proclaimed to all who have not yet heard of Your great grace in Christ Jesus.

Grant me sound rest tonight that I may arise refreshed and in good health tomorrow, ready to serve You in cheerful obedience to Your good and gracious will. Speak peace to my soul, for in You do I hope. Amen.

Thursday Morning

Another day is dawning;
Dear Master, let it be
On earth or else in heaven
Another day for Thee.

Gracious Father in heaven, I do not know when You will call me home—for in the middle of life we are in death. Regardless of the number of my days on earth, cause me always to be prepared to answer Your summons. I know that the road of my life leads finally to Your heavenly mansions above. Equip me for the trials and pitfalls that beset my way through life, and teach me to perform in Your holy name each duty that confronts me. Remind me daily that I am a pilgrim without a home here, and help me to assist my fellow travelers by sharing their burdens and showing them the glory of the life in You.

Whether my pathway leads to hilltops fair and high or through the sunless valleys where the shadows lie, it does not matter, for I know that You are with me and that underneath are Your ever-lasting arms. Where You lead me I shall gladly go. Oh, guide me unerringly on life's uncertain way here to my heavenly homeland there. In Jesus' name. Amen.

Thursday Evening

As this day closes, dear heavenly Father, I come to You to thank You for Your unfailing love, which even during the darkness of night continues to shine upon me and those I love. The wrongs and mistakes that have marred my life again today show me plainly how much I need You in my everyday life. Pardon me for Jesus' sake, and take away every impure thought and wish. Make my heart right, and make my actions reflect Your love. I want to become more like Jesus, Your dear Son, who went about doing good. Heal the sick, relieve the suffering, strengthen the weak, recall the erring, curb the wicked, help the troubled, comfort the sorrowing, and give peace to the dying. O Lord, who does not sleep, keep me safe until morning comes again. In Jesus' name. Amen.

Friday Morning

Almighty God and Father, the light of day calls me to the duties and privileges of the stewardship of life. Help me to be a good steward by revealing to me Your will for my life. May I make the best possible use of the talents that You have given me, so that I may always be ready to give an account of my stewardship.

In my activities today give me the wisdom to recognize whatever is evil before I am trapped by it. Grant me the strength to resist every temptation to sin and shame. Let me never be afraid to say, "How can I do this great wickedness and sin against God?"

Grant me the opportunity today to do good to someone who is in need of my love. When others deny You, give me the courage to confess my faith. Show me how to live in a manner worthy of Your holy name.

In Jesus' name I pray. Amen.

Friday Evening

O Lord God, I thank You that the knowledge of Your presence kept me from gross sin today, made me more gracious in dealing with my fellow human beings, and more zealous in performing the duties You have given me.

O Lord,
I need Thy presence every passing hour;
What but Thy grace can foil the Tempter's power?
Who like Thyself my guide and stay can be?
Through cloud and sunshine, oh, abide with me!

I pray, heavenly Father, that You would reveal Yourself especially to those tonight who are passing through trial and tribulation. Teach them to know that "ills have no weight and tears no bitterness, with Thee at hand to bless," and that nothing "will be able to separate us from the love of God in Christ Jesus our Lord."

Stay with me in the coming night, and let me hear You say to me: "Fear not, for I am with you; be not dismayed, for I am your God. I will strengthen you, I will help you. I will uphold you with My victorious right hand." Amen.

Saturday Morning

"O Lord, Thou hast searched me and known me! Thou knowest when I sit down and when I rise up; Thou discernest my thoughts from afar. . . . Even before a word is on my tongue, lo, O Lord, Thou knowest it altogether."

As I begin a new day with You, search my heart, dear Lord, and purify my affections so that I may love only those things which please You, and put You first in everything.

Help me to overcome the temptations I will meet today. Strengthen my faith that victory over the devil may be mine to Your glory. Keep me mindful of the sufficiency of Your grace, and let Your strength be made perfect in my weakness.

Give me the grace to guard against sins of the tongue, and preserve me from thinking evil in my heart against my neighbor. Teach me the joy of walking the ways of Your commandments, and bless those who walk in Your fear and favor.

Watch over me today when dangers overtake me, and ward off any evil of body or soul. If afflictions are to come to me this day by Your gracious direction, keep me humble and obedient to Your loving will.

Thank You, Lord God, for all Your past benefits and for Your promises of future mercies. Direct my day so that I may learn to praise You better tonight for the favors of today. Amen.

Saturday Evening

Lord Jesus Christ, Author and Finisher of my faith, I thank You for having brought me safely to the end of another week of my earthly journey to heaven. Praise and thanks be to You for having earned a perfect salvation for me, for bringing me to faith in You through the Gospel, and for having kept me in the true faith to this moment. Keep me in my baptismal grace so that I may, at the end of my journey, rejoice with all Your saints over the wonders of Your eternal love.

For the blessings of this past week I thank You, dear Lord, and pray You for Your mercies' sake to continue to deal graciously with me. Grant Your pardon for the sins by which I have offended You and hurt my neighbor.

Help me to look forward eagerly to the privilege of entering Your house of worship tomorrow. Grant me the grace to believe what I shall hear from Your Word, and give me the joy of offering to You the sacrifices of my praise.

Lord, You have opened my eyes to the beauty of Your grace. Close my eyes in rest, and let me see in the morning the sunshine of Your favor and the brightness of Your glory. Amen.

THE SECOND WEEK

Sunday Morning

Lord God, Father, Son, and Holy Spirit, grant Your sanctifying presence as I join my fellow Christians on this day in worshiping You in the beauty of holiness. "O Lord, I love the habitation of Thy house and the place where Thy glory dwells." "How lovely is Thy dwelling place, O Lord of hosts! My soul longs, yea, faints for the courts of the Lord. My heart and flesh sing for joy to the living God. . . . A day in Thy courts is better than a thousand elsewhere. I would rather be a doorkeeper in the house of my God than to dwell in the tents of wickedness."

Bless the preaching of Your Word in all the world today that many people of all races and nations may be brought to repentance and faith in Jesus Christ.

Bless my hearing of Your Word today that I may be confirmed in my faith and strengthened in my consecration to serve You. Keep me aware that I must be a doer of the Word and not a hearer only, lest I deceive myself.

All glory, praise, and honor be to You, the

Father, Son, and Holy Ghost, ever one God, world without end. Amen.

Sunday Evening

Heavenly Father, at the close of another day dedicated to You, I come before You with my evening sacrifice of prayer and praise.

I pray You that the blessings of today, hearing Your Word, singing Your praise, feeling Your presence, enjoying the fellowship of Christian people, may go with me in the week that lies ahead. Like this day of rest, so let also my days of work be consecrated to You.

I praise You for Your mercy and grace in Jesus Christ and for all the evidences through which You draw me ever closer to You with loving-kindness. I can never repay You for all that You have done for me. Accept, I pray, the praise of my lips and the dedication of my life.

For the coming night I commit myself into Your hands; let Your holy angels be with me that the wicked Foe may have no power over me. Amen.

Monday Morning

Dear heavenly Father, I thank You for having kept me safe during the night. Now I pause at the beginning of another week to ask You to go with me. I do not know what this week will bring—pleasure or pain, health or sickness, sunshine or shadow. However, I am not afraid if You will be my Companion, for You love me with an everlasting love and will guard and protect me from all evil. I need Your presence every step of the way. At the beginning of this week I ask only that You will stay close beside me, for, though I do not know what the future holds, I know who holds the future. Bless me in whatever I do. Make me strong physically, mentally, morally, and spiritually. Watch over me and over those I love. I ask this in the name of Your beloved Son, my Savior and Redeemer. Amen.

Monday Evening

As evening comes, I thank You dear heavenly Father, who created day and night, for the health and protection You have given me today. I do not deserve even the least of Your many blessings. For Jesus' sake forgive my sins and shortcomings, particularly if I have offended some soul weak in faith or if I have neglected the opportunity to lead someone to You. Grant me Your Spirit's power so that each day I may grow in faith and in the knowledge of my Savior.

Guard my home. Protect my family. Bless the friends I love. Look with mercy on all people. Comfort those who have experienced sorrow. Cause the Gospel of Your love in Christ to stir the hearts of all people. Grant me and all people a greater appreciation of Your mercy so that we may serve You more joyfully and eagerly. Be with me always. And now grant me restful sleep; for Jesus' sake. Amen.

Tuesday Morning

Lord God, my heavenly Father, at the beginning of this new day I ask You for the gift of Your Holy Spirit and the gift of a new spirit. As You have granted me protection from all danger through the night, be merciful to me and continue through the day to guard and keep me from every evil of body and soul, property and honor.

Open my eyes to every opportunity to do good, for You have created me in Christ Jesus to do good works and have appointed in advance that I should walk in them. Give me faithfulness for every task set before me, and grant me grace to serve all people as I would serve You my Lord.

Help me to live this day as though Jesus died yesterday, arose today, and were coming back tomorrow. Let His Cross be my glory and His favor my crown. Let His return to Judgment not frighten me but stimulate me to earnest attention to my faith and to faithfulness to Him.

Grant me enough success today to be encouraged

and enough difficulties to be humbled. Give me strength to overcome when I am tempted to do wrong and to seize my opportunities to do good.

> *Guide me, O Thou great Jehovah,*
> *Pilgrim through this barren land.*
> *I am weak, but Thou art mighty;*
> *Hold me with Thy powerful hand.*

> *Amen.*

Tuesday Evening

Lord Jesus, who welcomes all who come to You in a humble and contrite spirit, I lay before You the burden of my sins and ask You for Your gracious pardon. I have not done today all that You have asked me to do, and I confess my sins to You, who alone can cover my transgressions, and I pray You to remember them no more.

Help me to be stronger because of Your forgiveness, happier because of Your mercy, and more willing to serve You because of Your love.

Watch over me tonight, and favor me with refreshing rest and peaceful sleep. Should I close my eyes in sleep for the last time, awaken me to the brightness of Your glory and to the bliss of eternal fellowship with You.

You have been my Refuge and Strength, a very present Help in trouble. You have been my Shield and exceeding great Reward. How can I thank You for Your kindness, and how can I praise You sufficiently for Your mercies? Eternity will be too short, Lord Jesus, to utter all Your praise.

I commend myself, my body and soul, to Your safekeeping. You are faithful, and I trust in You. Amen.

Wednesday Morning

To You, O Lord, do I lift up my heart this morning, sincerely grateful for the opportunities of another day. Bless me in what I do today that all may be acceptable to You. Grant me such success in my work as You know to be best for me. Let me always remember that all depends on my possessing Your abundant grace and blessing.

Help me, I pray, to reflect in my life the infinite love with which You have loved me in Jesus Christ, my Savior. In all my dealings with other people help me to love them as I love myself, and to do for them what I would have them do for me.

Make me strong to resist any temptation to take what does not rightfully belong to me. Give me the courage to suffer losses rather than to inflict them on others. Help me to realize that life consists not in the abundance of things that I possess, but rather in what I do with what I possess, whether much or little. Teach me to know that godliness with contentment is great gain and to live accordingly.

In Jesus' name I pray, and in His name I begin my work today. Amen.

Wednesday Evening

Heavenly Father, I thank You for the privilege of speaking to You in prayer. It is good to know that I may come to You, the almighty Creator of all things in heaven and on earth, as my heavenly Father for Jesus' sake. Give me the faith of a loving child, never doubting that You will always hear my prayer. If sometimes You do not answer my prayers exactly as I have asked, then let me have the childlike trust to believe that You, heavenly Father, know best what to give me and what to withhold.

I thank You that You sent Your only-begotten Son into the world to redeem me from sin and death. Help me to live as Your child, avoiding sin and serving You with a consecrated life.

Take into Your special care tonight all those who are burdened with cares and crosses. Watch with the sick; comfort those who mourn the loss of a loved one. Reveal yourself to them as the heavenly Father to whom they may always go in time of trouble.

And now let me find rest and peace in refreshing sleep. In Jesus' name. Amen.

Thursday Morning

Dear heavenly Father, forgive my sins and help me, in gratitude to You, to forgive those who sin against me.

O Lord, my heart is by nature proud and unforgiving. It is hard for me to confess my sins, even to You. Help me to see clearly that I offend You daily and that, indeed, I deserve nothing but punishment. Help me to acknowledge freely that I am worthy of none of the things for which I pray, and help me to say with the Publican: "God, be merciful to me, a sinner."

My own struggles to be obedient to You remind me that others have similar struggles. Give them all believing hearts and help them so serve You. When they sin, make me as charitable toward them as You are charitable toward me, and help them find their way back to You. When they sin against me, give me an understanding and forgiving heart. Make me willing to forgive because You have loved me and forgiven me so much. When I sin against them, move them to forgive me, that together we may walk the way of life; for Jesus' sake. Amen.

Thursday Evening

Lord and Savior Jesus Christ, tonight I bring the needs of the church before You. I thank You for all

Christian churches and schools, for the teaching of the Gospel far and near, and for the messengers of peace who carry Your Word to mansions and cottages, to children and to higher schools of learning, to people of all races far and near, to rich and poor alike.

Inspire every member of Your church with Your Holy Spirit, Lord Jesus, that all may speak the things which they have experienced in their hearts. Help us to proclaim Your love for all sinners and the joyous faith that You are our God and Savior. Make eager witnesses of all believers, and give me the grace to speak Your Word when the opportunity arises.

Grant me Your grace that some soul may learn the way of life from me, that together we may rejoice with You in all eternity. Help me especially to witness to my relatives and friends and to the members of my own family.

And now, grant me peaceful rest, and renew my body and spirit for tomorrow. In rest and at work, gracious Lord, be at my side to strengthen, to guide, and to bless. Amen.

Friday Morning

Gracious Lord and adorable Savior, this morning I praise You who redeemed me through Your sacrifice on Calvary, thereby purchasing me to be

Your own. Grant that I may serve You with willing heart and untiring devotion to show my appreciation of Your great love for me. Make me an instrument of consecrated service to You that all I do today will give glory to Your holy name. Help me by Your grace and through strength coming from You to resist every temptation to sin; do not let me deny Your name or ever be ashamed of You. Enrich today with a genuine Christian joy and a sincere appreciation of Your goodness and Your peace, which fills the heart and mind through faith in Your redeeming Cross. Wherever an encouraging word is needed, let me give it. Whenever a helping hand is needed to lift a burden, make mine ready. Guide my footsteps in ways that are pleasing to You. May my whole day be dedicated to You, my Savior and my Shepherd. Amen.

Friday Evening

Lord, with grateful heart I come into Your presence this evening, mindful of Your many mercies that have enriched my day. You have forgiven me all my sins, comforted me in my disappointments, calmed me when irritated, and strengthened me in the face of temptations and doubt.

I praise You, Lord of heaven and earth, for Your goodness and Your grace. Grant that I may be faithful to You as You have been to me. You have poured out upon me blessing after blessing and have brought peace to my soul through the many promises of Your Gospel. Draw me closer to You with Your forgiving love. Bring to my heart that peace which has been purchased for me on Calvary through Your Son Jesus Christ, my Lord. Remove from my evening hours all worry and fear, that I may sleep under Your watchful care, knowing that all is well because You are with me. When the morning comes, let Your presence guide me through the day, mindful at all times that Jesus Christ is my Shepherd and Friend. Amen.

Saturday Morning

Lord Jesus Christ, Sun of Righteousness, shine into my heart and life today. Help me to reflect Your light that someone who does not yet know You as Lord and Savior may be directed to You.

I thank You that You have carried the guilt of my sins. Let the sin and evil that may threaten today have no power over me. Grant me the grace to recognize Your will and the faith to do it. In all my dealings with others today, let me be guided by Your precept: "Whatever you wish that men would do to you, do so to them."

Keep me united with You as a branch of the true Vine, that I may draw from You the strength to abound in good works. May You be glorified today in all that I do; for Your name's sake. Amen.

Saturday Evening

At the close of another week, O gracious God, I thank You that You have kept me from harm and danger of body and soul. I am grateful, too, that You have blessed the work I do. I am not worthy of all the goodness and of all the mercies which I have enjoyed in the past. Continue to bless me in body and soul with whatever is for my good.

In the quiet of this evening hour I would prepare my heart to worship You tomorrow in spirit and in truth. Bless the preaching of the Gospel in all the world that Your Word may accomplish what You desire, even the saving of souls bought by the precious blood of Jesus Christ.

Send Your Holy Spirit to the congregation where I intend to worship tomorrow. May the hearing of Your Word serve to strengthen my faith in You, the one true God, Father, Son, and Holy Ghost, and inspire me to true Christian living.

With the knowledge that You, heavenly Father, love me, I retire tonight safe in Your care and keeping. Amen.

THE THIRD WEEK

Sunday Morning

Lord God, merciful Father, I praise You for the light of this day, when by Your Spirit You will shine in my heart through the preaching and teaching of Your Gospel. Open my eyes that I may behold the wonderful truths of Your salvation and find new strength and hope in Your promises.

Bless the preaching and teaching of Your Word throughout Your church, and cause Your Gospel to fall as good seed on good ground that it may bear abundant fruit. Give power and conviction to Your ministers that their testimony to Your holiness and grace may ring clear and true to Your revealed Word.

Keep me from mere formality in my worship, from praying with the lips only while the heart is far from You, from failure to listen to the sermon with eager expectation as a message from You. Grant me the grace to bring my burdens to church and to leave them there at Your feet.

Guide Your wandering children to Your house today so that they may find true adventure in the abundant life which You have promised all who love You.

"Let the words of my mouth and the meditation of my heart be acceptable in Thy sight, O Lord, my Rock and my Redeemer." Amen.

Sunday Evening

Lord Jesus, by Your grace I have today accepted Your invitation: "Come to Me, all who labor and are heavy-laden, and I will give you rest." I thank You that by Your obedient life and innocent death on the cross You have removed the crushing burden of my sins. I praise You for the peace of mind and heart which You bestowed by Your promises of unfailing help and strength. I bless You for having made known once more the paths I am to walk in following after You.

Bless all those who made this day of worship meaningful and rewarding for me: my pastor, my Sunday school teacher, the organist, the choir, and my fellow Christians who gave me the benefit of their fellowship and prayers.

Help me this week to live Your Word. Bless the offerings I have brought for the extension of Your kingdom. By Your Spirit comfort those who could not for valid reasons be in God's house today.

"O Lord, I love the habitation of Thy house and the place where Thy glory dwells." Amen.

Monday Morning

At the beginning of another week of work I ask You, good Lord, to remember me in Your mercy and to look with favor on my activities.

Help me to be a better Christian this week. Strengthen my faith, increase my hope, and nourish my love for You and for all people.

Preserve me from pride, for You resist the proud and give grace only to the humble. Teach me to cast all my cares on You, for You have promised to care for me. Keep me from the love of money, lest I err from the faith and pierce myself through with many sorrows. Watch over me in moments of danger and temptation, and help me to do justly, to love mercy, and to walk humbly with You, my God.

I thank You for the opportunities to be a blessing to others and to be blessed by You this week. Let me rejoice at every chance to do good, and let me bear with patient forgiveness any evil done to me.

Do not give me tasks equal to my strength, but strength equal to my tasks. Grant me the grace to live today as though it were my last on earth and the first with You in heaven. Hear me for the sake of Jesus Christ, Your Son, my Lord. Amen.

Monday Evening

O Father of mercies and God of all comfort,

thank You for being gracious to me today. I have sinned against You, but You have not deserted me. Forgive me and cleanse me with the blood of Your Son.

Grant me a refreshing night of rest and sleep, and permit me to rise in the morning, ready to live another day to Your glory.

Watch over my loved ones near at hand and far away, refresh them with rest, and protect them with Your mighty hand.

As I have come another day closer to eternity, keep me in the true faith in Your Son as my only Redeemer from sin. Direct my thoughts and aims heavenward, lest I become too attached to the vanities of this life. Give me a sense of balance to enable me to rejoice in my earthly blessings without losing interest in my heavenly crown.

Look with mercy on those who are lonely, hungry, ill-clothed, or despondent tonight. Give me compassion to pity them and to help them in their need. Turn their hearts in faith to the Cross of Your Son, and give them pardon and hope. Make me thankful for my security in You, and let me be Your instrument in showing mercy to the needy. Amen.

Tuesday Morning

Gracious and holy God, I thank You for Your mercies which are new to me each morning. I am not worthy of Your many blessings and Your great love toward me. Often I have offended You. I ask You not to hold my sins against me, but to blot them out with the blood of Your beloved Son, who died for me. Help me to live more and more according to Your will. Make my thoughts charitable, my words kind, and my deeds selfless. Let my light shine before all people that I may glorify You and draw others to Your kingdom. Make me always humble and willing in Your service.

Oh, help me, Lord, this day to be
Thine own dear child—to follow Thee.
Amen.

Tuesday Evening

Again today You have blessed me, dear Lord, above all that I could ask or think. Accept my heartfelt thanks for Your loving care and Your undeserved mercies. You have permitted me to perform my tasks safe from harm and evil and have filled my life with Your generous bounties. Bless Your children everywhere. Comfort and help all those who look to You in need. Enlarge Your kingdom, and grant me grace always to confess Christ by word and deed. Pardon my sins, and let nothing come between You and me. Direct Your holy angels to watch over me and my loved ones wherever they may be. With the close of this day of grace, give me restful sleep so that I may awaken tomorrow refreshed and strengthened to meet the cares and problems, the tasks and opportunities, of another day. This I ask in Jesus' name. Amen.

Wednesday Morning

With grateful heart I rise to praise You, O Lord, my God, for You have refreshed me with a restful sleep and given me Your grace to see the dawn of a new day. You have also made this day. It belongs to You. Grant that every word I utter and every act I perform will reveal Your presence in my life. Make me thoughtful and considerate at work, and keep me patient with those who irritate me. Remove from my heart all malice and resentment, and enable me to bear quietly the unpleasant situations that I cannot change.

Protect me from all temptation, from doubt and worry, from lovelessness and strife. Throughout this day enrich my life with Your benedictions. Protect me from accident and harm, and bring me safely home tonight, for the sake of my Lord and Savior. Amen.

Wednesday Evening

As the evening shadows fall, closing out the light of the day, come, merciful Savior, with Your benedictions into my heart. Bring to me the full forgiveness of all my sins and grant me Your glorious peace which passes all understanding. Relax my body and give me much-needed rest. Remove all worrisome thoughts from my mind, and let me sleep undisturbed while You watch over me.

Bless all Your people far and near, and give healing and strength to the sick. If I have grieved anyone today, forgive me; if I have offended You, gracious Savior, blot out these sins; if I have been neglectful and thoughtless, make me different tomorrow.

Protect all Your children from want and worry, from bitterness and resentment, from strife and anger. Keep us all in steadfast faith, and give me the grace to resist every temptation to sin. Keep me humble and pure in heart. Hear my prayer, almighty Savior and Friend. Amen.

Thursday Morning

At the beginning of another day, Father in heaven, it is good to know that You have promised: "As your days, so shall your strength be." I cannot tell what today has in store for me, whether good fortune or misfortune. But I trust Your promise that You will give me the strength to bear whatever this day may bring; that You will make every experience work together for my good.

I am grateful for the opportunities that this day, with Your blessing, offers to provide the things I need. Teach me, while working for the material things of life, never to forget that my Savior said: "Seek first His kingdom and His righteousness, and all these things shall be yours as well." May spiritual values be first today in all that I think and say and do. Help me firmly to believe that You will give me the material things that You know are best for me.

Keep me faithful and true today to Jesus Christ and His religion, and may my conduct glorify Your name. Amen.

Thursday Evening

O eternal God, merciful Father, as the shadows of evening lengthen, I seek the comfort of Your gracious presence.

I thank You for all the blessings that I have enjoyed from Your bountiful goodness, for Your protecting care amid many dangers, for Your blessings on my work, for the love of the members of my family, for everything that has made this day a happy one in my life.

I am especially grateful for Your love toward me, for the forgiveness of my sins, for the assurance that You are my heavenly Father and Jesus Christ is my Savior, for the blessings of my church, and for Your grace, which has always been sufficient to sustain me.

"Bless the Lord, O my soul; and all that is within me, bless His holy name! Bless the Lord, O my soul, and forget not all His benefits, who forgives all your iniquity, who heals all your diseases, who redeems your life from the pit, who crowns you with steadfast love and mercy, who satisfies you with good as long as you live so that your youth is renewed like the eagle's. . . . Bless the Lord, all His works, in all places of His dominion. Bless the Lord, O my soul." In Jesus' precious name. Amen.

Friday Morning

Lord God, loving Father, keep me from temptation today. I know that Satan will not stay away from me and that the example of the evil world will entice me. I do not know what today's temptations today may bring. Keep me lest I am tempted to take Your name in vain, to take my work too easy, to lie, or slander, or steal. Preserve me from neglecting opportunities to do good in my work or at home.

Dear Lord, You know my sinful heart, which so easily departs from You. Give me the grace to recognize temptation when it comes, and fill my heart with Your Holy Spirit that I may resist and overcome sin.

Help me to regard the trials which may come to me this day as coming from Your gracious hand, that I may be drawn closer to You. Whatever the difficulties in my family or in my work may be, make me strong in hope and trust. Help me to say: "My heart from care is free; No trouble troubles me," knowing that troubles must fade in Your presence. Help me at all times to look forward to the day when I shall rise above all pain and trouble to the glorious mansions prepared for me by my Lord and Savior Jesus Christ. Amen.

Friday Evening

Merciful Savior, as the shadows of night lengthen and the darkness deepens, I commit myself and all my loved ones to You. Hide Your face from my sins, and forgive them for the sake of Your bitter suffering and death. Keep sorrow and harm from me tonight, and guard me against fear. Protect my dear ones who are far away, and guide them in a safe path.

O Lord, have pity on the sin-stricken, and comfort them with Your Word. Raise the fallen, cheer the faint. In some way bring the comfort of Your Word to all who will receive it. Let them find a word in Scripture for their present need, or send them a Christian messenger who will point them to You. Make all Christians willing to open their hearts, their voices, and their purses, that the Word of Life may be brought to all people.

Give me rest from my work today that I may awake with a strong body and an alert mind tomorrow, prepared for whatever the day may bring. Keep me thankful, hopeful, and cheerful, ever intent on serving You and my neighbor. Hear me, gracious Savior. Amen.

Saturday Morning

Gracious Father, Caretaker of my soul and Protector of my life, I come to You this morning, seeking Your guidance for the day. I need You every moment as I go about my work or seek my recreation during my leisure hours. Grant that I may give evidence by word and conduct of my loyalty to You and my devoted love to the Savior, who has redeemed me and brought me to faith that I may be a member of His church.

Give me the courage to lift high the banner of the Cross through the sincere profession of my faith and the high standard of my Christian life. Let my chief concern be to give of my time and thought and possessions to the building of my church. Permit nothing to keep me from worshiping You in Your sanctuary tomorrow and confessing Your Son as my Savior and Lord. In Your presence let me find forgiveness and peace. Help me to put You in the very center of all my interests for the sake of my adorable Redeemer, who died on the cross because He loved me. Amen.

Saturday Evening

As this week comes to a close, I praise You, Lord Jesus, with my grateful heart for the protection and guidance that I have enjoyed through Your goodness and love. Your continuous presence has made the day brighter. Even though I have failed and faltered, You have not turned from me. In Your loving-kindness erase each and every sin, and draw me closer to Your loving heart, where alone forgiveness and peace is to be found. Let not the sins of this day or yesterday cling to me. Then Yours shall be the praise and the glory.

Bless me tonight with a refreshing sleep that I may be fully alert tomorrow as I worship You in Your temple. Grant that the Lord's Day message may have a special significance for me, and that I, having heard it, may apply it to my life in word and action this coming week. Bless the preaching of the Gospel at all times and in all places, and bring many to hear the saving truth that You alone can set us free from the power of sin, most glorious Savior.

May the peace and the hope of Thy Gospel make us all better Christians, stronger in faith, nobler in character, more consecrated servants and faithful disciples. Stay with me this coming night in Your grace and mercy, divine Friend and Redeemer. Amen.

Sunday Morning

Heavenly Father, hallowed be Your name. Help me on this Lord's Day to come into Your presence with thanksgiving and to join my fellow Christians in hymns of praise and adoration. As I kneel before You, my Maker, give me joy in worship and help me to declare before all people that You are a mighty and forgiving God. Help me to give the glory that is due Your holy name. Graciously accept the offerings of my hands, and use my gifts in the service of my congregation and of Your church everywhere.

Fill my pastor with a rich measure of Your grace. Help him to speak Your Word courageously and convincingly, that the hearts of the hearers may be drawn closer to You. Send Your Holy Spirit into the hearts of people everywhere that they may believe and be saved from sin and damnation. Multiply the number of believers mightily, and give them the courage to confess You before all people. Give me and my church the grace to believe and teach Your Word in its true meaning, and help me and all Christians to pattern our lives accordingly.

By Your Holy Spirit make me pure in heart and mind, help me worship You in the beauty of holiness, and grant that in word and deed I may ever seek to please You. Above all else, grant me life eternal through Jesus Christ. Amen.

Sunday Evening

Gracious God, I thank You for the blessings of Your Word, through which new strength and comfort have come to me today. Keep me in Your care, and help me daily to rejoice in the forgiveness of my sins and in the new life and salvation that I have in You.

Lord God, heavenly Father, keep and protect me tonight, and strengthen me for tomorrow that I may serve You and the people around me cheerfully and well.

Lord Jesus Christ, make me grateful for Your holy, bitter, and innocent suffering and death, and lead me with Your gentle Shepherd's hand all my days.

Lord God Holy Spirit, keep me in the saving faith, and strengthen my love and trust that I may walk humbly and serve my God nobly.

O holy blessed Trinity, send Your holy angels to watch over me and over those near and dear to me. Grant us quiet, peaceful sleep and, if it please You, a healthy and joyful awakening tomorrow. If in Your good pleasure tonight should be my last on earth, receive me into Your heavenly glory, where I shall worship and praise You forever. Amen.

Monday Morning

Heavenly Father, Your kingdom come. "Thine, O Lord, is the greatness and the power and the glory and the victory and the majesty; for all that is in the heavens and in the earth is Thine; Thine is the kingdom, O Lord, and Thou art exalted as Head above all. Both riches and honor come from Thee, and Thou rulest over all. In Thy hand are power and might; and in Thy hand it is to make great and to give strength to all. And now we thank Thee, our God, and praise Thy glorious name."

Rule this world, Lord, by Your gracious and almighty power. Restrain the wicked, give the countries of the world honest and peaceful governments, and grant that righteousness and peace may prevail everywhere.

Rule Your church, Lord, and govern its teachings by Your holy Word. Bless the teaching of Your Word that many more people may learn to know and love You and that the believers may be strengthened in their faith and in their Christian life.

Rule my heart, Lord, and help me to grow in the knowledge and love of You day by day. Bless my work today, and bless honest labor everywhere. Make an effective witness of me, and use me to bring the good news of salvation to people near and far.

Rule the hearts and lives of everyone that Your good will may be done in all things; in the name of Jesus. Amen.

Monday Evening

Lord, I thank You for the blessings which You have graciously given me on this first workday of the week:

For safety in traveling to and from my place of work;

For health and strength to be useful;

For the completion of a task well done and for the approval of my superiors;

For the pleasant companionship of my associates in work;

For protection against the physical hazards that accompany my work;

For the food, clothing, and shelter that my labor has purchased for me;

For the opportunity to show myself as a Christian to those around me, and for the courage to speak for You;

For these and all other blessings I thank You.

Help me constantly to become a better worker. Help me to remember that I am serving not only myself but also You and my fellow brothers and sisters. Make me always willing to do a day's work for a day's pay, and to give more of myself to others. Give me a peaceable heart in my dealings with others. Help me to love them, and help them to love me, remembering always Your own great love for me and all people.

As I fall asleep, give me joy in my Savior Jesus Christ and the full assurance that in Him I have forgiveness of sins and eternal life. Amen.

Tuesday Morning

Lord, gracious and merciful, by Your Holy Spirit You have implanted in my heart an undying hope that promises rest after the struggles of this present life and an everlasting peace in the glories of Your eternity. Look with favor upon me and mercifully help me through the difficult times of my life. Be with me as I face the hardships and irritations of today, the temptations of Satan, and the sins and doubts of my own heart. Graciously take me by the hand and lead me hour after hour in the sunshine of Your grace. Direct my footsteps on the journey of life to render service to You and all people. Keep out of my day all harm and danger of both body and soul. Let me live continually in Your presence.

I pray for all those who are weary and burdened, for all who are discouraged, for all who mourn and weep, and for all who are lonely and distressed. Draw closer to them and to me with Your ever-renewing strength, and preserve us all in this saving faith to the end of days, through Jesus, my precious Savior and Friend. Amen.

Tuesday Evening

Lord God, my Father in Christ Jesus, I do not know what tomorrow has in store for me, but I am not afraid, because I have You. You have promised me Your continuous presence, and that is enough to know. I place myself in Your care tonight, certain that tomorrow You will be with me as I journey on, performing my work with gladsome heart and to the glory of Your precious name.

Save me from the follies and enticements of sin. Keep from my heart all envy, bitterness, resentment, and discontent. Make me see that each task laid at my door is a privilege, each duty an opportunity, and each assignment a challenge. Bless me with patience, thoughtfulness, and good will toward my fellow workers. May all that I do and say everyday give honor and praise to Your Son Jesus Christ, my Savior and Redeemer. As You are with me this coming night, let me be Yours forever. Amen.

Wednesday Morning

Your loving-kindness, O God Eternal, has given me another day of grace with all Your promises and benedictions. Grant that I may accept it with thankful heart and use each hour to the honor of Your name. Let not the many vexations of the day rob me of the cheerful and hopeful outlook of life that is mine because of the faith I have in Christ Jesus and in the many promises You have made to me in Your Word. When discouraged, let me come to Your throne in prayer and learn again that nothing can separate me from Your love through Him who was crucified for me, Your Son Jesus Christ. Abide with me throughout today, and keep me in Your grace, and keep me unharmed in body and soul. Forgive me every sin in thought, word, desire, and deed, and let this day be rich in service to You and all people.

Then my heart and lips shall praise You throughout the day for the sake of Jesus Christ, my Savior and the Lover of my soul. Amen.

Wednesday Evening

As the day comes to its close and I once more worship You, eternal Lord. My grateful heart comes to Your throne of grace with songs of adoration and praise. I bow to receive Your benedictions and acknowledge Your loving-kindness and guidance as You have blessed my work and protected my soul from gross sins. In Your goodness You have opened Your hand and have given me more than I need for today. You have drawn me to Your heart and forgiven me all my sin and enriched each hour of this day with Your heavenly peace and the eternal hope that is mine through the sacrifice of Your Son Jesus Christ, my Priest and King.

Bless me with an undisturbed sleep tonight, and let no one take me from Your protecting arms. Hear me as I plead, for the sake of my Savior, the Shepherd of my body and soul. Amen.

Thursday Morning

O Lord, my God and Father in Christ Jesus, I thank You for the protection of Your angels through the night, for the rest You have provided, and for the gift of another day to live for You.

Keep me humbly dependent on You for every good and perfect gift, for You are my Father, and I am Your child.

If it is necessary, send me trials and disappointments so that I may be humbled and kept free from vanity. When You afflict me, do not let me turn away from You in despair but remain faithful to You in the sure hope that You chastise those You love and scourge every person You receive.

Keep Your eyes always on me, O Lord, and my

eyes always on You. You have said: "The steps of a man are from the Lord." "Order my footsteps by Thy Word, and keep my soul sincere. Let sin have no dominion, Lord, but keep my conscience clear."

Let this day be a day of witnessing for You, my Father, and for Your Son, my Savior, in whose name I come into Your presence. Amen.

Thursday Evening

Heavenly Father, Your mercies were new this morning, and they did not fail me through the day. Praise and thanks be to You for being faithful to Your promises and unwavering in Your steadfastness. I am not worthy, Lord, for today I have been unfaithful and have wavered from the path of righteousness. Forgive me for the sake of the bitter suffering and death of my Savior, Jesus Christ.

Help me to thank You as much for my afflictions as for my blessings, for all come from You for my good and bring me closer to You.

If I have unknowingly wounded anyone today by word or deed, pardon me. If I have neglected opportunities to bear witness to You, forgive me. If I have loved the world too much and You too little, do not take Your Holy Spirit from me, but restore to me the joy of Your salvation.

As night closes in on me, surround me with Your protective strength and almighty care. Remove all fears and dispel all doubts from my heart, lest Satan rob me of some of the certainty of my salvation and the sureness of Your protection. Keep me steadfast in my faith, and preserve me unto Your heavenly kingdom. Amen.

Friday Morning

Dear heavenly Father, in whom we live and move and have our being, I thank You for last night's rest and for the opportunities which this new day brings. May I serve You faithfully and diligently. As I perform my tasks, help me to be considerate and kind to those with whom I come into contact. Remind me that all people are Your creatures and that You would have all to be saved. When things go wrong, do not let me despair but look to You for guidance. Teach me to consider not only earthly values but, above all, eternal values. I wish no greater honor than to be called Your child. Stay close by me, and watch over those I love. I ask this in the name of Jesus, who shed His blood on Calvary for my sins. Amen.

Friday Evening

Gracious Lord God, stay with me, for it is almost night and the day is over. I praise and thank You,

for Your goodness and mercy have protected me
again today and have brought me safely home to
my loved ones. Whatever I have done wrong,
forgive, dear Lord. If I have failed in my Christian
duty, if I have disobeyed Your Word, for Christ's
sake remove my sins from me as far as the east is
from the west. Let Your divine care surround me
and Your faithful disciples everywhere. Bless Your
church in its effort to bring the Gospel to all people.
Protect our country with Your power, and so direct
the affairs of all people that wars may cease and
peace rule the nations of the world. Grant this, dear
Lord, for Jesus' sake. Amen.

Saturday Morning

Dear Father in heaven, deliver me from evil. You
have promised: "No evil shall befall you, no scourge
come near your tent," and yet I know that "through
many tribulations we must enter the kingdom of
God." Help me therefore to know that all things
work together for good to them that love God.

I know that You will keep evil from me according
to Your promise. Grant me Your grace that I may
not bring evil on myself by sinning. Spare me from
evils of body and soul, of property and honor.
When troubles arise, use them to strengthen me and
to draw me more securely into Your loving arms.
Bless me in my work and in my home according to

Your good pleasure. Make me patient in suffering, helpful to the afflicted, and grateful for all the blessings that You have given me. Show me ways of using my talents and powers for You and all people near and far.

Finally, when my last hour comes, lead me safely through the valley of death to the glory of heaven, where You will forever wipe away all tears from my eyes.

Yours, O Lord, is the kingdom and the power and the glory forever. Do what is best for me and for Your kingdom. Make me content. I know You will do it for the sake of my Savior Jesus Christ. Amen.

Saturday Evening

Lord, I thank You that You have given me health and strength to conclude another week in Your service. I thank You for all Your undeserved blessings, for my work, for my family, for Your daily care and protection, for Your Word, for peace of mind, for my church, and for my country. Help me daily to remember that all these blessings come from You and that without You I would be miserable, hopeless, and helpless.

Grant me Your care and protection tonight. Give me refreshing sleep in preparation for blessed worship of You tomorrow in company with fellow believers. Keep me and all others in Your paths tonight, particularly the young. Protect them from the sins and follies by which Satan tries to ruin their lives.

Preserve our country in peace. Guard our church against indifference and false teachings, and make our schools nurseries of useful knowledge for the young. Comfort the sorrowful, provide for the poor, and use me according to Your good pleasure in carrying out Your work on earth. Show me the needs of others, and move my heart to works of charity and love.

Each week and each day draw me closer to You through saving faith in Jesus Christ, and when this life is ended, receive me into Your eternal glory. Amen.

ADDITIONAL PRAYERS

Sunday Morning

Dear heavenly Father, who on the first day of the week created light out of darkness, I thank You that You have brought me to see the light of another day. Be with me and bless my visit to Your house today. As I hear Your Word, clear the darkness of sin from my heart, enlighten my understanding, and quicken my spirit. Create in me a spirit to praise Your name and to let my light shine before all people.

Blessed Savior, who on the first day of the week rose from the grave as my Redeemer from sin, help me with repentant faith to accept Your forgiveness, daily to rise from sin and to serve You in newness of life.

O Holy Spirit, who on the first day of the week descended on Your church with blessing and power, bless me with spiritual healing, and give me strength to speak the things I have seen and heard.

O holy, blessed Trinity, grant Your faithful pastors grace to preach Your Word with power. Preserve the hearers from distracting thoughts and cares. Enable me with open mind and ready heart to receive Your truth and to order my life according to Your Word and will; for Jesus' sake. Amen.

Sunday Evening

Accept my thanks, Lord God, for the joy and peace of Your Gospel message, for the physical rest, the mental refreshment, and the Christian fellowship which I have enjoyed today. Let neither care nor pleasure retard the growth of the seed of Your Word planted in my heart. Help me to put in practice the sacred truths I have heard. Forgive every thoughtless word or deed with which I may have offended You or my neighbor. Never permit the image of Christ to be marred in me through sin or shame.

Keep me and my loved ones from harm and temptation tonight. Grant me restful sleep, and awaken me refreshed in body and spirit tomorrow to meet the challenges of a new day. Give me strength and courage by my speech and conduct to set others a good example as I walk the Christian way of life to Your glory and for the sake of Jesus Christ, who went about doing good. Amen.

Morning Prayer

Heavenly Father, give me this day my daily

bread. With all people and with all Your creatures I look to You for all my needs. I pray You, care for my soul and for my body according to Your grace and wisdom.

Give me food, drink, clothing, and shelter in the measure in which it is good for me, and make me wholly content. Continue to give me health and work that I may earn my daily bread. Give me a generous heart that out of the abundance that You provide, I may help the needy.

O God, I pray You also, bless and prosper the members of my faith and my friends. Give us a government which rules for the welfare of all. Protect our country, our churches, our homes, our schools, that we may work quietly and enjoy Your blessings in peace. Help us all to remember that our needs will be supplied as long as we rely on You and on Your bountiful mercy. For all things make me thankful; in the name of Jesus. Amen.

Evening Prayer

Gracious Father, as I look back on the day which is drawing to a close, I have every reason to be thankful. I have kept my faith, and by Your grace I have been able to avoid falling into shame and disgrace. I have come through the day strong in body and mind, and Your blessing has accompanied my work.

But, dear Father, I have also every reason to be ashamed. My thoughts were not always with You as they should have been. Though my outward actions may have pleased people, there has been so much pride and selfishness in my heart that I can only say: "Make me more like You!" I have missed opportunities to speak of Your love for all people, partly because I did not watch for opportunities and partly because I was too fearful.

O God, forgive all that has been wrong with me, and draw me closer to You. Strengthen my faith and courage, and make tomorrow a better day for me, a day of thanksgiving and service, a day of joy and witnessing, a day of looking heavenward; through Jesus Christ. Amen.

Morning Prayer

Eternal Father, in Your fellowship is health and in Your grace is forgiveness and peace. By Your goodness I have life, and through Your mercies I am sure of my eternal salvation.

Take from my mind all worries and anxious thoughts, and remove from my day the irritations which make for discontent. Break to me enough bread each day, and fill my heart with the earnest desire to obey Your will and follow in faithfulness Your Son Jesus Christ, my Savior.

Remove all sin from my imperfect heart, and

keep me humble and trusting in Your grace. Put my mind at ease as I lean upon You as the Rock that is higher than I. As I go through the day performing my routine tasks and duties, let me find joy in the things I do, remembering that I am to glorify You in all that I say and accomplish. Bless me and those around me. Grant that I may return unharmed to my home to enjoy the benedictions of Your love. Then my thankful heart will sing the praises of Your goodness and mercy throughout the evening hours, through Jesus Christ, my Lord and my Redeemer. Amen.

Evening Prayer

Lord of heaven and earth, my understanding Father through our adorable Savior, You have so graciously made me Your own. I praise You, for Your mercies have been greater in number than the countless sands of the many seas. You have removed the burden of my sin, cleansed my conscience from the sense of guilt, comforted me in every frustration of the day, instructed me in Your Word, warned me against the deceitful enticements of Satan, and ordered my footsteps in Your ways of peace and joy.

I lift my heart and voice in thanks and praise to You and ask You to continue to be with me tonight. Preserve for me Your Word, the Gospel, which keeps me in Your grace. Feed both body and soul in Your kindness and love. Put my mind at ease, removing all worries and anxieties from my life. Bless me with restful sleep, and when I awake, I still shall be praising You, who art my loving Father in Christ Jesus, Your Son, my crucified Savior. Amen.

Saturday Morning Prayer

As I begin this day, I thank You, O Father of all mercies, for the blessings of this week now drawing to a close. You have again kept me from harm this night. Also during the past week You have granted me health and happiness. You have forgiven my sin, strengthened my faith, and nurtured my hope of heaven. For these and countless other blessings I am grateful to You.

I pray You, in Your mercy accompany me and my loved ones on our path of duty. At work or at leisure, help me to keep myself unstained by the world, so that with pure heart, kind words, clean hands, and ready feet I may daily grow in Your service.

Heal the sick, restore the erring, help the troubled, support the afflicted, and comfort the sorrowing. Bless our government, and prosper our nation.

Keep Your Word constantly before me that it

may ever be a lamp unto my feet and a light unto my path. And if I should be called upon to bear a cross, grant that the love of my Redeemer, who gave Himself for me, may give me strength that I may not falter under the load. Stay with me to journey's end. I ask it in Jesus' name. Amen.

Saturday Evening Prayer

As the shadows of night settle upon another week, I thank You, my loving heavenly Father, for Your merciful guidance and protection in the past, Your comforting assurances for the future, and the eternal bounties of Your grace.

According to Your mercy forgive my failures, and help me more and more to abound in that faith which works through love. Grant Your sustaining presence to me and to all those who are in need.

Bless our home, our church, our nation. Give our missionaries zeal and courage to proclaim Your name boldly before all people. Protect our loved ones in the Armed Forces. Grant quiet and rest and peaceful sleep tonight.

In the morning let me arise refreshed in body and spirit for the services of Your house, there to sing Your praises and to be built up in my precious faith. Into Your hands I commend myself and all people for help, guidance, protection, pardon, peace, and life eternal; through the everliving Christ. Amen.

Prayers for Christian Living

For More Abundant Living

Blessed Lord and Savior Jesus Christ, You have warned me that "a man's life does not consist in the abundance of his possessions." Teach me to realize that happiness in life does not depend on the measure of material things I may call my own, but on the use I, as a good steward, make of what You have committed to my care.

Grant me the grace to desire not so much an abundance of goods but rather an abundant life of service to You and to all people. Show me how to use Your gifts, both spiritual and material, that my life may bring happiness to me and be acceptable to You.

Bless, dear Savior, the work I do for Your kingdom. Grant me the joy to see the fruits of my labors and of my offerings. Make Your word, "Give, and it will be given to you," true also in my experience that I may be able to continue in the abundant life.

Someday, I pray You, let me hear You say to me, "Come, O blessed of My Father, inherit the kingdom prepared for you from the foundation of the world." Amen.

For Purity of Heart

O Lord God, who delights in a clean heart, I do not come relying on my personal righteousness, but trusting solely in the merits of Your beloved Son, my Redeemer Jesus Christ. For His sake forgive me my sins. Create in me a clean heart, and renew a loyal spirit within me. Remove from my mind all evil desires. Cast out from my life all greed and envy, all anger and hatred, all pride and vanity. Spare me from an accusing conscience. Fill my soul with love for You and a spirit of service to all people. Grant me strength to resist and overcome temptation. Clothe me with the garment of righteousness that Jesus won for me on Calvary. Cause me to grow in grace before You and to increase in works of love as long as I live. And when my life comes to a close, give me a place with You in heavenly glory. This I ask in Jesus' name. Amen.

For Readiness to Forgive

Lord Jesus, I ask with Peter of old: How often must I forgive those who sin against me and offend me? O Lord, if I am to forgive seventy times seven, then You must give me the grace and the will to do so. My sinful heart is resentful and often filled with bitterness against others. So often I have been hurt and sinned against. I must confess to You, Lord

Jesus, that I do not find it easy to forgive and forget. Help me, O Lord.

I know You have forgiven me times without number. That is why I am coming to You, asking for help. Enable me in all sincerity of heart to say as You did on the cross: Father, forgive them; and then help me to forgive as You have forgiven me more than seventy times seven.

Hear my plea, gracious Lord. Amen.

For Finding Peace of Mind
Through Forgiveness

To Your Father-heart I come today, Lord God, seeking peace of mind. I am distressed and perturbed, irritated and worried. I am dissatisfied with myself and the world around me. My sinful heart is rebellious, my day is filled with envy, and my feelings are so easily hurt. I know, O Lord, that I am at fault. I have not opened my heart to You, nor have I given service and consideration to those with whom I live in this home and to those with whom I must work throughout the day. Everything annoys me, I must confess. Those with whom I work get on my nerves. O God, I admit that it is I, my sins, my lovelessness, which create these situations. Therefore, I come to You, asking You for grace to conquer myself. Restore to me the desire to walk in Your presence, and let me live in the sunshine of Your love.

Forgive me all my sins, and fill my soul with peace. Go with me, Lord, through the day, put my mind at ease, and speak peace to my soul through that reconciliation which is found in the Cross of Jesus, my Savior. Amen.

For Finding Joy
in My Forgiveness

Blessed Father in heaven, You are abundant in goodness and truth, forgiving iniquity, transgression, and sin, I thank You for the grace and mercy assured me by the redemption of Your Son. In Your fatherly love look down on Your disloyal child. "Cast me not away from Thy presence, and take not Thy Holy Spirit from me. Restore to me the joy of Thy salvation, and uphold me with a willing Spirit." Have mercy on me for Christ's sake, and forgive what I have done wrong and what I have left undone. Quiet my troubled conscience with the knowledge of sins forgiven. By faith in Christ fill my heart with the joy of adoption into the family of heaven. Engraft me as a living branch upon Your Son, the Vine, that I may bring forth fruit in abundance by leading a holy and blameless life to the glory of Your name and for the benefit of all people. Help me ever to live in Your favor and finally to die in Your peace; for the sake of Jesus Christ, my Lord and Redeemer. Amen.

For Overcoming My Worries

Lord God, my heavenly Father, who has made all things by the Word of Your power, I, Your unworthy creature, give You praise and honor. Though the immensity of Your creation overwhelms me, You have assured me of Your infinite and continuing love. In Your mysterious mercy You have seen fit to give Your only Son into death for my sins that I, believing in Him, might become Your adopted child and an heir of eternal life.

As I struggle with my petty problems and am troubled by the worries that beset my pathway through this world of sin, grant me the assurance that You are my loving Father and I Your cherished child by faith in Christ. Free me from the anxieties of life. Lift me up from the depths of despair. Give me grace to accept the forgiveness You have provided for repentant believers. Cause me in the middle of every difficulty and trial, every sorrow and woe, to trust Your providence and to look to You alone for help. And make all things work together for my everlasting salvation; through Jesus Christ, my Lord. Amen.

For Overcoming My Fears

Lord God, heavenly Father, "whom have I in heaven but Thee? And there is nothing upon earth that I desire beside Thee. My flesh and my heart may fail, but God is the Strength of my heart and my Portion for ever."

I am deeply grateful that You are my God, who has promised never to leave me or forsake me. I trust Your Word that nothing shall be able to separate me from Your love which is in Christ Jesus, my Lord.

I am ashamed to confess that sometimes my heart is filled with fear as I look at the trouble and turmoil in the world today. Sometimes I am afraid to face a difficult problem in my personal life. Forgive my little faith. Increase my faith in Your loving-kindness and in Your almighty power that I may overcome my fears and meet every trying experience with confidence. Make Your strength perfect in my weakness.

By Your Holy Spirit enable me confidently to say, "I fear no evil, for Thou art with me." In Jesus' name. Amen.

For Overcoming My Doubts

Lord, I am troubled by many things, and sometimes I fear for my faith. In my sorrows I am inclined to forget You and in bodily weakness I sometimes doubt Your ability to help. In health and prosperity I am inclined to forget You and to ascribe my successes to myself and to my hard and intelligent work. I know that all this shows weakness of faith, sinful pride, and forgetfulness of You. I must say tearfully: "I believe; help my unbelief."

Gracious Father, help me always to remember that You are God; that You have given me my body and soul, my food and clothing, home and family, and all that I have; that You defend me against all danger and guard and protect me from all evil; not because I deserve it, but because of Your fatherly goodness and mercy.

Help me always to remember, Lord Jesus, that You are true God and a true human being; that You have shed Your holy precious blood for me to redeem me from sin, from eternal death, and from the power of the devil, that I might be Yours forever.

Help me always to remember, Lord God, Holy Spirit, that You have called me by the Gospel and brought me to faith in my Lord and Savior Jesus Christ, that I have forgiveness of sins and eternal salvation through such faith, and that You have promised to keep me in the saving faith until my dying day.

Yes, Lord, help me to remember what You have graciously done for me, and in that remembrance help me to trust in You for all my needs, never doubting that You are my God and that I am Your beloved child. In that knowledge help me to live joyfully and confidently, and to die gloriously; through Jesus Christ. Amen.

For Overcoming My Disappointments

Lord God, heavenly Father, You have promised that all things work together for good to them that love You, to them who are called according to Your purpose. You have made me Your child and an heir of this promise. Strengthen my faith in Your perpetual mercy and unfailing care. Forgive me for doubting Your faithfulness and for questioning Your love. If You rewarded me according to my sins, surely my lot in life would be nothing but misery and continual heartache. But You are gracious and forgiving, You bless me in spite of my sins.

Help me to understand that my disappointments are not a result of Your neglect but rather Your call to repentance and a closer walk with You. Continue to correct me when I fail You, and keep my eyes upon the crown of glory reserved in heaven for me.

Help me to use my disappointments as occasions for prayer and for humble dependence on You, who, together with the Son and the Holy Ghost, are the only true God and eternal life. Amen.

For Overcoming My Dissatisfaction

Lord God, life seems to hold and offer so little to

me from day to day. Everything angers me, and my friends seem to be so thoughtless and unconcerned about me. Nothing seems to satisfy me, nothing gives me pleasure. Everything, Lord, is boring and irritating. I know, God, it is I. I need help. My outlook on life must be changed. You, Lord God, are the only one able to do this. Therefore, I seek You and ask You to enter my heart and take full possession of me that I may by Your grace overcome my depressed moods. Give me full measure of contentment and patience. Create in me a greater willingness to forget self and to be helpful to others.

Let me find in the many promises of Your Word the key that will open the door to a more satisfying and richer life. Remove from my heart all jealousy and selfishness, and show me how I can be a blessing to others and helpful to the discouraged. Forgive me for complaining, and help me to count my blessings day after day. Make me appreciate Your benedictions, and keep me in Your grace. In You and in Your Son, Jesus Christ, my Savior, let me find my most complete joy and contentment and peace. Help me, O Lord. Amen.

For Overcoming My Sensitiveness

Dear Savior Jesus Christ, I am troubled by a serious personal fault that makes life hard for me and for those around me. I know that You have redeemed me from sin and damnation and that this is reason enough for me to be kind, cheerful, hopeful, and helpful. Yet I am much too sensitive in my daily dealings with relatives, friends, and with associates in my work. I often regard every adverse word or criticism as an insult. As a result, relations are often strained, and life is a burden instead of a glorious adventure.

I do not want to be like that, Lord. I want to be like other people. I want to be able to take the irritations of life calmly. I know the fault is mine. I am proud when I should be humble, selfish when I should be helpful, depressed when I should be cheerful. I make life miserable for others when I should be kind and helpful.

When I look at You, my Savior, who was reviled but did not revile, who was despised but did not despise others, who was abused but who served others in life and in death, I am thoroughly ashamed of my childish, selfish behavior. Turn my heart, and make me what I ought to be. Give me a new outlook that I may rejoice in the welfare of others, spend my life in the service of others, and be a blessing wherever I go.

Lord, when I think what You did for Saul the Pharisee, for Zacchaeus the tax collector, and for countless others, I know that You can also make me a pleasant and useful person whom others will be glad to have in their company. I trust You to do it, merciful Savior. Amen.

For Overcoming My Self-Pity

Lord, I know that I am easily hurt and feel myself slighted and passed by as I meet associates at church and at the many social gatherings in the community. It seems as though no one cares for me. Therefore I feel sorry for myself and think that I am mistreated and ignored. Lord, help me to overcome this unhealthy outlook on life. Create in me a deeper interest in my fellow beings. Let me look away from myself and seek to be useful to others. Grant me the grace to be less self-centered and self-conscious. Forgive my murmurings, and make me cheerful and friendly.

I know I am precious in Your sight, for You have given Your Son as a sin offering for me. You, O Lord, are thinking of me and of my eternal welfare. Grant that this truth will help me to conquer my self-pity. Do not let me continue to complain about my lot in life. Open my eyes to see that where I am I can serve You and be of real service to all people. You have called me by name. I am Your own. May I rejoice daily to know that my name is written in the Book of Life. Let me count my blessings as an heir of salvation. Give me the satisfaction of sharing with others the saving truths of the Cross and telling them of Jesus, the Savior, who sacrificed His life that they, too, might be Yours through all eternity. Abide in my heart for the sake of Jesus, my Savior and Friend. Amen.

For Overcoming My Intolerance

Lord God, heavenly Father, You know that I love You. I pray You in the name of Jesus Christ to make me understand that if I love You, I must love my neighbor too.

The world around me is often indifferent toward the poor, and prejudiced against those of another race or color. Erase from my heart all thoughts of pride and prejudice, and give me a spirit of tolerance and good will toward all.

Help me to be more than merely tolerant. Help me to love those who are in need of my love—no matter who they may be. Keep me aware that You have created them all of one blood to live on this earth, and that You have sent Your only-begotten Son into the world that "whoever believes in Him should not perish but have eternal life." Forbid that I should ever by an intolerant word or deed offend anyone You have loved and for whom Your Son, the Savior, has died. Teach me, by Your Holy Spirit, to be more like You with every passing day in loving my neighbor of another race or color.

Let the spirit of humility and tolerance increase

among all people that we may live together in this world in peace and good will. In Jesus' name I pray. Amen.

For Relief from Frustration

Gracious God, who searches the hearts of all people and knows all of their thoughts, "create in me a clean heart, O God, and put a new and right spirit within me. Cart me not away from Thy presence and take not Thy Holy Spirit from me. Restore to me the joy of Thy salvation and uphold me with a willing Spirit."

Teach me to say with the psalmist: "Why are you cast down, O my soul, and why are you disquieted within me? Hope in God; for I shall again praise Him, my Help and my God."

"Search me, O God, and know my heart! Try me and know my thoughts! And see if there be any wicked way in me, and lead me in the way everlasting."

If my frustrations arise from a rebellious and dissatisfied heart, forgive me, Lord. If my restlessness arises from my failure to look to You for rest, teach me to come to Jesus with my cares and lay them at His feet. If those who dislike me succeed in making me miserable, help me to rise above this pettiness and be strong in You and in the power of Your might. If You are testing me, give me the strength to endure my test, for You have carried the burden of my sins for me. Help me to know the godliness with contentment that comes from You alone, for Jesus' sake. Amen.

For Grace to Adjust Myself

Gracious God, heavenly Father, I must confess that I am sometimes upset by the many changes that come in life. I find it difficult to make the necessary adjustments. I do not ask to understand, but help me, I pray You, always to realize that no matter what happens to me, and what changes must be made, You still love me and will make every experience work together for my good.

Give me the faith to trust Your promise, "My grace is sufficient for you." In mercy forgive all grumbling and complaining of which I have been guilty in the past. Teach me to follow the example of Jesus, my Savior and Lord, who in trial and tribulation said, "Not My will, but Thine, be done." In that spirit I shall be able to meet whatever life has in store for me. For Jesus' sake. Amen.

For the Grace of Humility

Most righteous and everliving God, whose standard is perfection and whose justice punishes sin with consuming fire, I bow before Your majesty and humble myself in Your holy presence. Make me understand that the way of the sinner leads to eternal disaster. Impress Your will on my heart. Grant me true repentance. For Jesus' sake forgive my sins and shortcomings, my ignorance and hardness of heart. Give me grace to pattern my conduct after Your Word. Destroy in me the spirit of pride. Make me realize the seriousness of my sin so that I may humbly throw myself on Your mercy. Preserve me from the spirit of the Pharisee who would make himself more important than others. Help my heart to be merciful to all people. Enable me out of sincere gratitude for sins forgiven to crucify my flesh and to excel in Your service. And by Your mercy grant that I may finally enjoy the light and joy of heaven; for the sake of Jesus Christ, Your Son, our Lord. Amen.

For Grace to Be Patient

Divine Savior, how patient You have been with me! Too many times I have failed You, yet You have not turned from me, but with compassion You have sought me and drawn me to Your forgiving heart. How thankful I am that You have tenderly pleaded with me through Your Word and Your Christian church! Grant that I may learn from You to be patient with others, thoughtful and considerate, even though they irritate, upset, and disturb my peace of mind. Remove from my heart all resentment toward those who provoke me by word and action. Do not let me return evil for evil, unkindness for unkindness, harsh words and caustic comments.

When You, gracious Savior, were mistreated, misunderstood, hurt and bruised in body and sorrowful in soul, You prayed: "Father, forgive them." Grant me the grace to face the many vexing problems of the day with patience and find in You rest and peace and contentment. Let me lean on You for strength and guidance and abide Your time, Savior and Lord. Amen.

For the Grace of a Consecrated Life

O Lord, my God, You have said: "I have redeemed you; I have called you by name, you are Mine." Praise and thanks be to You for having loved me with an everlasting love and for having drawn me to You with loving-kindness. You did not spare Your Son, but delivered Him up to the cruel death of the cross that I might be Your own and live under You in Your kingdom. What shall I give to You for all Your benefits to me?

Lord, give me a thankful heart and daily determination to live like Jesus, who died for me and rose again. Help me to live my thanksgiving by reverent and cheerful obedience to Your will and by unceasing trust in Your loving-kindness and unfailing mercy.

Help me to be what You want me to be, and when I fail, forgive me for Jesus sake. Let Your daily pardon strengthen my daily will to love You and all people.

O Lord, You called me out of darkness into Your marvelous light. Give me the grace to live as a child of light and an heir of heaven, that others may glorify You and be drawn to Him who is the Light of the world, Your Son, my Lord. Amen.

For the Grace
to Be True to Myself

Dear Father in heaven, I thank You for all my blessings of body and mind. Help me to make the most of them, and help me to be myself, which I often find hard or impossible. Too often I want to be someone else, to imitate others, forgetting that You want me to use my talents as You have given them.

Teach me to recognize that my failure to make the most of myself is often due to jealousy or to a mistaken sense of values. I want to do as my neighbors do, though my earthly means do not permit me to live according to their standards. The outward glamour of certain people or occupations sometimes causes unrest in my heart. Sometimes I aspire to be what I cannot or should not be. I sometimes lose my sense of gratitude for what You have made me and given me, and as a result I become unpleasant or unhappy.

Help me first of all to understand myself, Lord. Help me to see who I am and what I can do, and then give me the courage and endurance to develop my talents and powers and to be wholly myself. Help me to see Your beauty and wisdom in the diversity of talents and powers, and help me and others to use the diversity of gifts which Your gracious hand has given for the joy and benefit of all people.

Yes, Lord, help me to find myself and to develop myself that I may serve the purpose for which You have created me. Above all, strengthen my faith and trust in You that I may remain Your child in all eternity; through Jesus Christ. Amen.

For the Grace to Make the Right Decisions

Heavenly Father, you know all things and see the end from the beginning, You are never at a loss as to what to do next. The wonders of Your creation and the miracles of Your all knowing direction of the affairs of all people and nations testify to the infinite wisdom with which You order all things.

I humbly confess that I am often confused by the problems of my life. Sometimes I do not seem to know which way to turn. I pray You, therefore, to enlighten me by Your Holy Spirit that I may recognize what is Your will in every situation; give me the courage to decide every issue accordingly and to leave the final outcome to Your direction.

I especially thank You, heavenly Father, that Your Spirit has brought me to make the right decision concerning You, my God and Savior. I have been richly blessed in the faith that You are my heavenly Father and that Jesus Christ is my Savior. Keep me firm in this faith to the end, and then give me, according to Your promise, the crown of life. For Jesus' sake. Amen.

Gratitude for the Blessings Received

Heavenly Father, Your goodness has opened Your hands to supply me with the needs of today, and Your love has protected me from harm and danger and injury. But You have done more; You have opened Your heart and drawn me closer to Yourself with Your forgiving mercies. Truly, You are wonderful, O God, merciful Father! Make me thankful every day for Your many blessings. Let me count them one by one with a grateful heart. May I never forget Your benefits when a desire of my heart has not as yet been granted. Too often I have forgotten to thank You for everyday blessings. I arose this morning and could walk; I opened my eyes and could see; I reached for my food and could enjoy it. O Lord, Your blessings are many. Who could count them all?

But how often I have forgotten to thank You for peace of mind, for cleansing from sin, for the air we breathe, the refreshing water we drink, the beauty of Your creation which we can behold! Lord, make me truly grateful and appreciative as I count my blessings each and every day. Above all, I thank You that You have given me a Savior who walks with me, cleanses me from sin, and guides me daily in the paths of righteousness. In Your grace let me live today with thankful heart, for Jesus' sake. Amen.

Gratitude for Special Blessings Received

Almighty and eternal God, of whom and through whom and to whom are all things, I join my voice with the chorus of the angels and the glorified saints assembled around Your throne in ascribing to You blessing and honor and glory and power.

I am unworthy of the least of Your blessings. And yet in Your mercy You have given me life. By the precious blood of Your Son You have called me into Your kingdom at my Baptism. You have redeemed me. You have sanctified me by Your Spirit and renewed me in Your image. You daily and richly forgive all my sins. Without number, O Lord, are Your spiritual blessings.

I am also richly blessed with material goods. You have given me health, surrounded me with the beauties of Your creation, supplied me with friends and loved ones, and endowed me with wonderful personal gifts and abilities. You have singled me out for special blessings not shared by others. I have not always recognized or appreciated them as I should. Teach me to remember them and to count them one by one. Help me daily to place them at Your feet and to dedicate myself anew to Your service; for Jesus' sake. Amen.

Gratitude for the Joy of Being a Christian

O God, I thank You for the saving faith in Jesus Christ, my Savior, and for the privilege of being a Christian. Give me a deep and abiding faith, and grant me the grace to show in all my actions and in all dealings with others that You are the Ruler of my heart and mind and that the joy of salvation is the dominating influence of my life. Keep me from becoming discouraged by the troubles and cares of this life, and make me trusting, cheerful, and confident. At the same time keep me humble always in the knowledge that salvation is from You and that heaven is Your gift.

In gratitude for the salvation which You give, help me to live and die in the spirit of the psalmist: "I will extol Thee, my God and King and bless Thy name forever and ever. . . . Great is the Lord and greatly to be praised, and His greatness is unsearchable. One generation shall laud Thy works to another and shall declare Thy mighty acts. On the glorious splendor of Thy majesty and on Thy wondrous works I will meditate. . . . The Lord is gracious and merciful, slow to anger and abounding in steadfast love. The Lord is good to all and his compassion is over all that he has made. . . . My mouth will speak the praise of the Lord, and let all flesh bless His holy name forever and ever." Amen.

For Conquering Alcoholism

Lord Jesus Christ, You are the Strength of my soul, and in You do I hope. Without You I can do nothing, but all things are possible for those who trust in You.

Give me the grace to see my sins of drunkenness as rebellion against Your holy will, as a crucifixion anew of You, and as a wounding of Your Spirit, whose temple I am. Cut away from me all satanic webs of self-defense and pitiable excuses, and help me cry: "Wretched man that I am! Who will deliver me from this body of death?"

Give me the faith to lean only on You. Strengthen my trust in Your grace, which is sufficient for my weakness. Bestow Your strength on me when my will power fails. Guard me when I am tempted, and give me the power to resist my sinful appetite for strong drink. In Your name I ask it. Amen.

Prayers for Christian Worship

For the Joy of Worship

Heavenly Father, let me share the joy of the psalmist who said, "I was glad when they said to me, Let us go to the house of the Lord." May every opportunity offered to worship You in Your house find me eager to join in hearing Your Word, in singing Your praise, in lifting up my heart to You in prayer.

May Your Holy Spirit so bless the hour of worship in Your house that I may be refreshed after the toils and burdens, the sins and failures of the weekday world. I need so much my Savior's invitation, "Come to Me, all who labor and are heavy-laden, and I will give you rest."

Teach me to come into Your presence with a contrite heart, and let me depart with the knowledge that my sins are forgiven. Fill my spirit with the peace which the world cannot give.

> *From Thy house when I return,*
> *May my heart within me burn,*
> *And at evening let me say,*
> *"I have walked with God today."*
> *Amen.*

Before Going to Church

Gracious Savior, You have made each Sunday a day of triumph through Your resurrection, increase in me the desire to worship You as my adorable Lord and merciful Savior. Grant that the message of Your redeeming love, which I shall hear today, may make me more appreciative of Your grace, strengthen my faith, ennoble my character. Make me more faithful in this coming week that I may be able to resist all temptations that come my way. Make me ever more willing to serve others as You have served me. Remove all distracting thoughts from my mind, and let me apply all that is said to myself rather than to others.

Let my attendance at Your house of worship be an example to others that they, too, may come and share with me the peace and hope which are mine through Your Gospel of love and grace. Pour out on me Your richest blessings now and always, most gracious Savior and Friend. Amen.

After Attending Church

With thanks and praise in my heart, O Lord, I return from the service where I have worshiped You today, confessed Your name and my faith, and made my prayers. You have spoken to me through Your Word, assuring me of the forgiveness of all my sins. These promises sent me on my way rejoicing as my heart is filled with peace and the certainty of salvation. You have shown me the way that I should go, warned me against the pitfalls of sin, and given me directives for my Christian living. Grant that I may daily practice the things that I have heard. Let Your Word bring forth in me abundant fruit to the glory of Your name.

Bless the ministry of my pastor. Watch over all the members of my church, and lead them daily in the paths of righteousness. Help me to dedicate myself to You in a richer and fuller service and share with my fellow Christians the responsibility placed upon us by Your Son Jesus Christ.

Open more doors of service to me, and let me enter gladly and serve You with all the ability You have given me by Your goodness and love.

Bless me daily with Your benediction, and let Your presence guide and protect me throughout this week. In Jesus' name I ask this. Amen.

For Baptismal Grace

Lord God, heavenly Father, You have redeemed me, You have called me by my name and have said: "You are Mine."

Praise be to You for having received me as Your child in Holy Baptism. Thanks be to You for having washed away all my sins, for making me a partaker of all the blessings of Your grace, and for bringing me to faith in Your Son through this washing of regeneration and renewing of the Holy Ghost.

By Your Holy Spirit keep me in my baptismal grace. Arouse me daily to heartfelt contrition and repentance so that I may never spurn Your grace through indifference and unbelief. Stir me up daily by this grace to a life of holy obedience to Your will.

In my moments of temptation and doubt cause me to rest my hope upon the grace bestowed on me in Holy Baptism. You will always remain faithful to Your responsibilities as a heavenly Father. Keep me faithful to my responsibilities as Your child. When I fail, do not throw me aside, but for the sake of Your Son and my Savior pardon me and help me to improve. Keep me in Your grace until I meet You face to face. Amen.

For My Communion Sunday

As I desire to approach Your table, precious Savior, make me worthy and acceptable, mindful that Your grace alone gives me the privilege to partake of this blessed Sacrament. I have sinned, I have been discouraged, I have given way to needless worries, I have questioned Your promises, I have had a doubtful mind. I confess all these and other shortcomings and ask You to receive me neverthe-less and to blot out all my sins against You and all people. Create in me a clean and pure heart, a greater faith, and the grace to walk with You in that way which leads to life eternal. Draw me to Yourself with Your constraining love, and send me on my way rejoicing because of the forgiveness and peace which I have received at Your table of love and grace. Preserve me in this union with You and the fellowship of those with whom I have shared this blessed meal. Continue to be with me and all Your people until journey's end, most gracious Savior and Lord. Amen.

For Bible Sunday

"Thy Word is truth," gracious Lord and Father, the only truth which makes us wise to salvation through faith in the crucified Savior. I praise You, Lord God, for this revelation of Your love and the saving Gospel of my redemption through Jesus' blood. May nothing be more precious to me than Your Word. May I at all times reach for my Bible when I need guidance and counsel, comfort and strength, healing and forgiveness. Help me to grow in understanding and knowledge of Your revelation and feel at home with Psalms and Prophets, Gospels and Epistles.

Grant that the number of those increases who daily read Your Word and find through Christ of Calvary peace of heart and mind and directives for

Christian living. May I at all times speak of this hope which is in my heart and continue to grow in knowledge of You and Your will; for Jesus' sake. Amen.

For a Better Understanding of My Bible

Gracious Lord, I thank You for Your Word of salvation, for it is a lamp unto my feet and a light unto my path. Grant that I may love it, understand it, believe it, and live according to it.

Make the Bible my comfort and guide. Open my heart and mind when I read Your Word that its sacred message may take root and grow. Help me to regard all faithful pastors and teachers as Your representatives, and strengthen my faith through their preaching and teaching.

Teach me to regard Sunday not only as a day of rest from my labors, but also as a day on which I may gladly hear and learn Your holy Word.

Help me today, and at all times, to seek and find You as You have revealed Yourself in the Scriptures. Grant that I may daily worship and glorify You as my Creator, my Redeemer, and my Comforter; through Jesus Christ. Amen.

On Joining the Church

Dear heavenly Father, who through Your Son Jesus Christ has brought me into sonship with You,

I thank You that You have led me to the knowledge of Christ as my Savior and through Him introduced me to the larger fellowship of the Christian church. Now that I have become a member of the church, help me to be faithful to my baptismal vow, diligent in the performance of the duties I have undertaken, and steadfast in my associations with my fellow Christians.

Give me grace, I pray You, to be an effective witness of my faith in word and deed. Preserve me from any lapse of my discipleship. Because I have received greater knowledge, enable me to render greater service to You and to all those with whom I may come into contact. Cause me to be an active, energetic builder in Your kingdom, not for self but for Your glory and the salvation of precious souls. Inspire me to let my light shine here until I shall see the light of Your glory there. Grant this for Jesus' sake. Amen.

Taking an Office in the Congregation

Lord Jesus, Bishop and Head of the Christian Church here on earth and King of kings on the throne of eternity, my congregation has honored me by choosing me to serve You in a special capacity of our congregational life. The ability to perform my duties well and acceptably comes from You and depends upon Your benediction. Give me a ready heart and willing hands and a truly Christian vision to grasp each and every opportunity to serve You, confess You as my Savior, and serve all people within and without the church.

May I at no time forget that I am rendering this service to You, and am not merely to please people. Let me experience daily the satisfying joy of doing things for You. If it be Your will, grant that I may also see the fruits of my labor. Allow nothing to discourage me or rob me of this zest and zeal which is put into my heart by Your Holy Spirit. Preserve in our congregation the unity of peace, that with one accord we pursue the tasks that lie before us. Then Yours shall be the praise and the honor and the adoration from my grateful heart, now and always. Amen.

For New Year's Day

At the dawn of this new year, precious Savior and divine Lord, I desire to begin today in Your name. Therefore I ask You to take full possession of my life, hold me by the hand and lead me from day to day, protecting me from all dangers of body and soul. Shield me from the temptations of sin and remove every doubtful thought from my mind. Let not the worries and fears of the future rob me of that peace of mind which is mine through Your sacrifice on Calvary. Order my footsteps in the paths of righteousness, and keep me in Your grace.

Abide with Your children wherever they are, and help them through their trials and troubles. Forgive us, one and all, our many sins of the past through Your cleansing and precious blood. Grant me and all that love You the strength to live victoriously every day.

Give to Your church, eternal Savior, continued growth, and prosper the work of our hands as we seek to win souls for You. Bring this saving Gospel to many more. Preserve peace among the nations that Your message of reconciliation may not be hindered in its progress as missionaries go from place to place. Let me live in peace with all people, avoiding discord, strife, and hatred. Give me an unwavering faith in You as my Savior and King. Make this year another year of grace to me and to many, for Your name's sake. Amen.

For the Epiphany of Our Lord

O gracious God and Lord, who by a star led the Magi to see the manifestation of Your love for all people in the Christ Child, I thank You for this revelation that the whole world should share in the salvation which You have prepared in Jesus Christ, Your only-begotten Son.

Enable me by Your Spirit to find peace and joy in the faith that I, too, have been redeemed by Jesus

Christ from sin, from death, and from the power of the devil. Let me never forget that I am now Christ's own and that it is my duty to live under Him in His kingdom and serve Him in righteousness all the days of my life.

Graciously reveal Yourself to all people who even now do not know Jesus Christ and salvation in Him. Gather Your elect from all the nations of the world that Your house may be full, and Yours shall be the kingdom and the power and glory forever and ever. Amen.

For the Lenten Season

Gracious God, Father of my Lord Jesus Christ and also my dear Father, I thank You that You have permitted me to see another Lenten season, during which I am privileged again to meditate on the Cross of Christ with its many comforting spiritual lessons. May this holy season bring me rich personal blessings. Cause the message of the slain Lamb of God to impress on my heart and mind the awfulness of my sins and to lead me to Calvary for pardon and peace. Lead me to see that my sins caused His great agony in the Garden; that my sins nailed Him to the Cross of Calvary; that He was forsaken by His own that I might not be forsaken by You; that He died so that I might not die eternally.

O Lord Jesus, grant that especially during this sacred season the story of Your wondrous love for me may draw me closer to You so that in gratitude for Your great love I may rejoice in my redemption, walk with You in willing obedience, and follow Your example of love and sacrifice.

O Holy Spirit, during this Lenten season grant all pastors a double measure of Your outpouring to arouse the indifferent listeners, to stir up the lukewarm, to encourage the timid, to assure the doubting, to calm the disturbed, and to console the sorrowing. May troubled souls everywhere by the message of Lent be led to sincere repentance and trusting faith in the Cross of Calvary, so that, dying to sin, they may live to You now and forever. In Jesus' name. Amen.

For Palm Sunday

Lord Jesus Christ, Lord of lords and King of kings, on Palm Sunday in the long ago the multitudes at Jerusalem nailed You with their glad "Hosanna to the Son of David! Blessed is He who comes in the name of the Lord! Hosanna in the highest!" But a few days later the people shouted their angry "Crucify Him! Crucify Him!" O God, forbid that I should ever be so unfaithful to You.

Abide in my heart, Lord Jesus, and rule as my Lord and King. Enable me, I pray You, by Your

Holy Spirit to remain steadfast in my loyalty to You. Keep me from presumptuous sins, lest I crucify You anew with unholy living. Above all the temptations of the unbelieving world, let me hear Your gracious promise, "Be faithful unto death, and I will give You the crown of life."

Hear my prayer, Lord Jesus! Amen.

For Good Friday

O Lamb of God, slain for sinners, this day brings me to the foot of Your Cross. Humbly and shamefully I admit that You have carried my griefs and sorrows; the chastisement of my peace was upon You, and with Your stripes I am healed. I thank You that You suffered all as my Substitute.

For me You endured the treachery of Judas; the mockery and mistreatment of Herod; the miscarriage of justice before Annas, Caiaphas, and Pilate; the scourge, the rod, and the crown of thorns. For my sins Your hands and feet were pierced with nails, Your lips tasted of the vinegar and gall, Your side was pierced by the spear.

Here I behold the tremendous price of my sins that cost You Your life, Lord Jesus. Here I see You as the Lamb of God, who by one sacrifice has forever perfected them that are sanctified. May Your Cross ever be the source of my forgiveness, comfort, joy, and peace.

As I again view You today suspended on the cross of Golgotha, may I by Your love be prompted to say with Paul: "I have been crucified with Christ ... and the life I now live in the flesh I live by faith of the Son of God, who loved me and gave Himself for me." Bless the preaching of Your Cross everywhere, and by its constraining love draw all people to You that they may live with and for You forevermore. For Your holy name's sake I ask it. Amen.

My Easter Prayer

Lord Jesus, risen and everliving Savior, with Your people of all ages and races I adore You as my Lord and my God, who has crushed Satan's head, conquered sin and death, and redeemed all people from the forces of evil. Accept my hallelujahs as I rejoice with believers, saints, and angels because You have come forth triumphantly from the grave to live forevermore. I ask You to cleanse my heart from all sinful desires and dwell there with Your eternal peace. I rejoice to know that You have blotted out all my transgressions and reconciled me with Your Father in heaven, that I as a child of His household may seek His face and know that He is full of tender mercies and boundless compassion.

I praise You because of the hope that You have brought to my heart. I need not be afraid of death and dying because there is condemnation for us who believe in the saving power of Your Cross. To all who are sorrowing let this Easter Day bring the comfort of Your promises and a new joy of expectancy as they look forward to the day when they shall be reunited with their loved ones in the eternal glory of heaven.

I rejoice today because I know that Your church shall go on from victory to victory, receiving strength from Your almighty hand. Even the gates of hell shall not prevail against Your church. Accept my vows of allegiance this day as I dedicate myself anew to Your service.

Take full possession of my heart, remove all sin, scatter all doubts, drive away all worries. Let Your Spirit set aglow in me a love that will not die. Increase in me day after day the desire to follow You to whatever place You shall lead me, until I stand before Your Throne to behold Your glory as the risen Lord, and praise You with saints and angels with an undying and perfect love. Hallelujah. Amen.

The Ascension of Our Lord

Lord Jesus Christ, who was delivered unto death for my offenses, raised again for my justification, and crowned in glory at Your ascension, I praise You for having finished the work given You by Your Father for my redemption and my coronation.

As once Your disciples gazed steadfastly into heaven as You ascended on high, lift my eyes heavenward and set my affections on the eternal treasures reserved there for me. You have ascended on high and have led captivity captive; I pray You to take fuller possession of my soul, my life, my all, so that I may look constantly to You as the end and aim of my life.

Strengthen in me the longing for fulfillment of Your promise: "Where I am, there shall My servant be also." Keep me in the true faith, so that I may always be prepared for Your second coming and return to Judgment, ready to meet You in the clouds of heaven when You return in glory to take me to Your glory.

Let Your ascension strengthen me in the assurance of my ascension on high, and lift me above the cares and worries of this life. Until You return, give me the grace and joy of knowing that You rule all things for the ultimate well-being of Your dear children. Grant me the cheerful readiness to submit myself to Your mighty protection and loving direction, and help me daily to crown You as my Lord by a life of holy obedience to Your will. Amen.

For Pentecost Sunday

O Holy Spirit, who on the great day of Pentecost descended on the apostles and set their hearts on fire with Your blessings, I pray You to enter my heart daily through Your Word and stir me up to wholehearted devotion to my Lord and Savior Jesus Christ. Open my lips to testify to the living hope which You have begotten in me through the risen Christ. Give me courage and boldness to speak Your Word with power so that more people may know the Father, the Son, and You.

Bless the preaching of the Gospel everywhere, and through it conquer the hearts of all people for Christ, their King. Graciously attend the work of Christian pastors and teachers throughout the world that by their ministry many souls may be added daily to Your church. Grant zeal and understanding to Your church so that the people of God may be warmed to greater service to all people.

Enlighten my understanding, control my affections, purify my ambitions, and sanctify my actions, that others may see my good works and glorify my Father in heaven. Keep me repentant over my sin and trustful in my Savior. Comfort me in my afflictions, and preserve me from any sin whereby I might grieve You. O Holy Spirit, enter into my heart with Your blessings and into my life with Your direction. Amen.

For Trinity Sunday

Eternal Lord, who has revealed Your majesty,

glory, and greatness as Father, Son, and Holy Spirit, I fall before Your throne with angels and saints of the ages in awe and wonderment. You are a great God and *my* God and Lord. I come to You, heavenly Father, in the humble faith created in my heart by Your Holy Spirit. In that saving faith in Jesus, who has redeemed me through His Cross, I am Yours by grace. Accept my adoration and praise, my "Holy, holy, holy," and touch my lips and heart and make them clean. I confess that You are the only revealed God and have spoken to me through Your Word and Your Son Jesus Christ.

Preserve me in this saving faith, and give me the grace to confess You and Your Son and the Holy Spirit as my God. Let me never be ashamed of You nor deny You. Keep my soul from sin, and let me live daily in the sunshine of Your love.

Then throughout eternity my lips shall praise You, Your grace and Your majesty, as Creator, Redeemer, and faith-preserving Spirit. Amen.

For Mother's Day

Dear heavenly Father, You have said through Your prophet, "As one whom his mother comforts, so I will comfort you." I thank You for Your infinite love which so exceeds human understanding that to make it more real to me You compared it with a mother's love for her child. On the strength of this assurance, I know that I shall have Your constant guidance, help, support, and protection.

On this day, set aside to honor mothers, I thank You especially for the gift of Christian mothers. Bless them always. Give them grace to set a good example for their families. Make them constantly aware that their children are a sacred trust from heaven. Hold Your protecting hand over them, and give them strength for every job, courage for each trial, and trust in You that each day grows stronger.

I thank You particularly for the gift of *my* mother and for her love, which has often comforted me. I ask You to help make me worthy of it. May I never do anything that would grieve her heart. May I always follow the path that she has charted—the path which leads to You. Guide our footsteps that we walk in the love of Jesus, who set an example by His love for His mother. This is our prayer in His name. Amen.

For Father's Day

Gracious God, Father of my Lord Jesus Christ, and through Him also my true Father, I thank You that You have given me an earthly father. As Your representative he has provided me with all that I need to support this life on earth, and he has also given careful attention to my immortal soul.

On this day, set aside for honoring fathers, I pray

You to impress all fathers with their responsibility as parents. Help them in holiness and industry to provide for the physical needs of their families. And grant them grace to rear their children in the way of Your blessed Word.

I pray You, make me increasingly aware of the great debt I owe my father. Help me to cherish him as Your precious gift. May I always honor him with my love, my respect, and my devotion. Do not let me leave from the paths of righteousness in which he has led me from infancy. Cause him as a Christian father to find happiness in my attempts to translate his directions and example into a life of unselfish service.

Finally, when life's day is done, grant me the joy and bliss of spending eternity with You, my heavenly Father, and with him, my earthly father, as well as with all my loved ones.

In Jesus' name I ask it. Amen.

For Reformation Day

Lord God of hosts, who is the Refuge of every sinner and the Strength of all who put their trust in You, I praise You for having allowed me to share in the blessings of the Reformation.

Without any merit or worthiness on my part, You have sent Your Holy Spirit into my heart and brought me to faith in Your dear Son, Jesus Christ.

You have made known to me the worthlessness of my own good deeds and the perfect merit of Christ. You have directed my faith away from the commandments of men and caused me to rest my hope only and solely on the exceedingly great and precious promises of Your Gospel. You have revealed the beauty of Your grace, which rescued me from a just condemnation and assured me of certain salvation in Christ.

Grant me Your grace that I may receive Your forgiveness with thanksgiving and reflect Your mercy in thanks-living. Use me as Your witness in bringing the message of pardon in Christ to people everywhere.

Open my eyes to a better understanding of Your Word and a deeper appreciation of Your grace that my faith in Christ Jesus may grow and flourish with the fruits of righteous living.

Grant purity of doctrine and practice to Your church that everyone may be rescued from all human errors and be led to all truth by Your Spirit. Hear me for the sake of Him who is the Way, the Truth, and the Life, Your Son, my Lord. Amen.

For Thanksgiving Day

With a heart full of appreciation because of Your goodness and with thanksgiving in my soul for Your boundless grace, I come on this national day of thanksgiving, God of loving-kindness and mercy, to join with heart and voice all the people of this country to praise and adore You as a wonderful God and understanding Father in Christ Jesus. Throughout the year You have opened Your hands and poured out on me blessing after blessing. You have provided me with all that I need to sustain body and life. You have opened Your heart and drawn me closer to Yourself, blotted out all my sin, cleansed my conscience from guilt, and spoken peace to my heart. Richly and abundantly You have offered to me Gospel and Sacrament, that my soul be healed, my faith strengthened, my character developed, and my life directed. Accept the thanks and praise of my grateful heart. I sing of Your goodness, I shout for joy because of Your mercies.

Let my thanksgiving, however, go beyond words and give evidence in the sharing of my blessing with the hungry, the needy, the lonely. Give me the grace to continue to praise You as a thankful child of Your love and with all the family of Your household to serve You with faithfulness and loyal devotion through Jesus, my Savior and Friend. Amen.

For Christmas Eve

Almighty God, heavenly Father, I thank You for Your unspeakable gift to mankind in the birth of the Christ Child at Bethlehem, as announced by the angel this holy night. May the mystery of the Word made flesh fill my soul with wonderment and yearning that like the shepherds I may hurry to worship at His manger bed. Change my heart from a busy inn that has no room for Your Son, that it may be a quiet chamber kept for Him.

Help me in the spirit of true repentance to rejoice in my Savior's birth that in genuine faith I may join in the song of the angels, share the delight of the shepherds, and adore Him with the Wise Men. Grant that Christ may be born again to me this holy night that the truth, love, and redemption He brought may henceforth abide in my heart and life. Like Mary, may I keep all these things and ponder them in my heart always.

And as You have made me a partaker of His glory here, grant that I may share His glory there. In Jesus' name I ask it. Amen.

For Christmas Day

O God the Father, I praise You for the gift of Your Son, who was born in the poverty and lowliness of Bethlehem so that I might enjoy the riches of your grace and the exaltation of sonship with You.

O God the Son, I adore You for humbling Yourself to be my Savior, for bearing my sins in Your own body, and for rendering to my Father in heaven a perfect satisfaction for my sins.

O God the Holy Spirit, I glorify You for having made my heart a home for the Savior of the world and for bringing the peace of forgiveness to my soul through faith in Him who is the Prince of Peace.

O blessed Trinity, on this holy day give me a humble and contrite heart that I may joyfully claim the Babe of Bethlehem as my Lord and my God. Remove from me the tattered robes of my own righteousness, and adorn me with the spotless garment of Christ's righteousness.

Use every gift received this day from loving friends to remind me of the gift of a Savior so that my heart may rejoice and my tongue can sing, "Glory to God in the highest!"

Help me to cradle the Christ Child in my heart, O Holy Spirit, and give me the grace and strength to love and adore Him all the days of my life. Amen.

For New Year's Eve

Heavenly Father, daily Caretaker of the souls of all people, put protecting arms around me as I enter this new year of grace. Guide me safely through harm and danger that may come my way, protect me from accident and sickness, and preserve me in that saving faith which will make me more than victor over all temptations, doubts, and unbelief.

Tonight I am mindful of my many sins and

transgressions and ask You to erase them, every one, by Your love and mercy through the precious blood of my redeeming Savior. In Your loving-kindness draw me closer to You that I may walk with renewed determination and strength in Your paths of righteousness, where peace of mind and the hope of heaven are my treasures and my joy.

Preserve in our community Your saving Gospel and prosper the work of the church established by Your Son, Jesus Christ, my Savior, that the community and the ends of the earth may know that there is no other name which saves but that of Your Son, our crucified Savior and Lord.

You, O God, have been good to me through the years, and in Your mercy You have forgiven me my sins day after day. Grant me the grace to continue steadfast in this saving faith and to walk as a child of Your family, through Jesus Christ, my eternal Redeemer. Amen.

For the Pastor

Lord Jesus, Chief Shepherd of the sheep, I thank You for giving our congregation a pastor who is faithful and true. Keep me grateful to him—

> For preaching Your Word in truth;
> For his fellowship in the Gospel;
> For his influence in our community;
> For the example of his Christian life.

May I always be aware of my obligation to pray for my pastor, to honor him, and to support him in his ministry among us. Bless him and continue to make him a blessing to me and to the work of Your kingdom.

Help my pastor and the people of our congregation to be devoted to the faith, and at last take us all to the Church Triumphant above.

I pray in Your name. Amen.

For the Congregation

I am grateful to You, Lord Jesus Christ, that You have established Your church on earth, where You bless me with love and mercy in the Word and the Sacraments.

I am grateful that Your Word is proclaimed in our congregation in truth and purity. May the Holy Spirit fill the members of our congregation that it may be said of us "they devoted themselves to the apostles' teaching and fellowship, to the breaking of bread and the prayers." Help me to do my part to keep it so for my own spiritual good.

Use our congregation for the building of Your kingdom on earth. Make our congregation a power for good in our community, and bless our efforts to bring Your saving Gospel to the unchurched, to the glory of Your name.

Hear my prayer, O Jesus. Amen.

For the Sunday School
and Its Classes

Lord Jesus, Friend of children, who has commanded Your church, "Let the children come to Me, do not hinder them; for to such belongs the kingdom of God," we pray You to look favorably on the efforts of our congregation to bring up our children in the nurture and admonition of the Lord. We commit our Sunday school, its teachers and officers, its pupils and visitors, to Your divine care and guidance.

Grant, we pray You, Your blessing to the instruction offered in our Sunday school. Cause its teachers always to be impressed with the importance of their work, since theirs is the privilege of molding souls for eternity. Give them wisdom and grace to teach the way of salvation in such a clear and compelling fashion that our children, whom You have bought at the price of Your holy blood, may be ready and eager to receive it. Help them also by personal virtues and exemplary lives to support the instruction they give in the classroom.

Since You alone can give the increase, we ask You dear Lord, to cause the good seed of Your Word to bring forth abundant fruit in the hearts and lives of our Sunday school children. Give them ready and teachable hearts. Cause them to seek their Creator when they are young. Make them full of faith, hope, and love. And, having been trained in the way they should go, may they ever abide in it, and even when they are old never leave it. Grant this for Jesus' sake. Amen.

On Opening of School Term

Gracious Father, I thank You for the schools of learning which are opening their doors for another term. Bless the millions of children and young people who are beginning a new school year, and fill them with a love for learning and with a desire to develop their powers to serve You. Bless their teachers with true wisdom and with love for You, and keep them from teaching anything which might harm the proper moral and spiritual development of the students under their care. Make all schools nurseries of useful knowledge, and fill all educators and students with a deep sense of devotion toward You.

Hold Your protecting hand especially over the Christian schools of our country and the world. Give the teachers in these schools a deep insight into Your saving Word, and make them effective witnesses for You, convincing teachers of Your Word, and wise counselors to the immature. May their testimony and teaching bring peace and comfort to countless hearts. May their example strengthen the students in their determination to place themselves in Your service. Increase the number of Christian schools and teachers, and make them an ever greater power in the building of Your kingdom.

Help students and teachers to see all knowledge in relation to You. Grant that they may use their knowledge in developing the resources of the earth according to Your will and for the benefit of all people. Give us all the true wisdom which finds its joy in You and in the salvation which we have through Jesus Christ. Amen.

By the Teachers of the Church

Lord, Thy blessings are so rich and many that I find myself overwhelmed in thinking about them. I thank You that You have permitted me to become a teacher in the church. Help me to perform my work quietly and unselfishly. Help me to prepare my lessons with only the thought of serving You and of leading souls closer to their Savior. Help me to appreciate Your blessing and guidance more and more.

Bless the work of all teachers in the Sunday schools and in other classes of Christian education. When they become discouraged, lift their tired spirits; when they experience difficulties in their work, lead them to happy solutions; when they see little result of their work, remove the curtain from their eyes and show them the rich fruits of their labors; and at all times keep them humble and cheerful in their work of love.

Lord, in all things guide the instruction of our youth, and give all who have a part in it a right spirit of consecration and love. Grant that their instruction may be heeded, to the salvation of many souls; through Jesus Christ. Amen.

By the Youth of the Church

Dear Father in heaven, who loves young and old and who cares for them all, I thank You for Your unwavering love and the mercies which come to us day by day. Together with all believers I adore You and praise You as the Lord of all and the Savior of lost mankind.

At this time I pray You especially for myself and all the youth of the church. You know the many temptations that come to young people. Though Satan may smile at us, he does so only to deceive us. Though the world seeks to charm us, it does so only to mislead us. And even our own hearts are sinful and unclean, as are the hearts of all people. I pray You, therefore, show me and all young people a special measure of Your grace, and lead us in right paths.

Help us grow in the love and use of Your Word. Help us find godly friends and companions who will support and uphold our Christian faith. Give us an understanding of what is right. Move our hearts to want to do what is right, and crown our desire to serve You with fruits of godly action. Guard us against the temptations of youth, against irreverence, pride, lust, disobedience, and dishonesty. Turn our hearts to You and our thoughts heavenward. Give us a faith that rises above ridicule and a courage that overcomes any obstacle which may be placed in the way of our faith. Strengthen us in Christ, and keep us with Christ until the day when we shall see You face to face in the full radiance of Your glory. Amen.

By the Youth Workers

Lord Jesus, the Savior of old and young alike, I thank You for the youth of the church with their faith and enthusiasm, and for the mature people who guide the young. I pray You, give faith to both young and old, obedience to Your Word, and an earnest desire to serve You.

Look with favor on me and on all youth workers, especially on the youth workers in Your church. Help us to understand young people better, to guide them toward the achievement of their hopes and aspirations, to teach Your Word in ways that are meaningful to them, to set for them a good example, to counsel them wisely, and in every way lead them on the paths that You have walked.

Give us patience when it seems young people do not respond to our training efforts. Help us to remember the impulses and desires of our own youth, that we may better understand the people with whom we work. Make us charitable, helpful, kind in all things. Give us a self-sacrificing spirit, even when our labors may seem thankless, that the youth of the church may be preserved in the faith, that converts to Your name may be won, and that the future of the church may be secure. Hear me, gracious Savior. Amen.

By Camp Workers

Lord God, Creator of all life and beauty on earth, I thank You for all the gifts of Your love. Help me more fully to appreciate the bounty that You have given, and help me to impress others with Your marvelous goodness.

As a camp worker, I am to help others see the beauties of nature. I am to lead them in various forms of recreation and in other camp activities. Give me the skill I need to do the work at hand. Give me a creative mind, and help me develop ideas and programs through which Your name will be glorified and through which the campers will be led to greater appreciation of You and to greater love for You.

Help all with whom I work and play to enjoy

nature and to find spiritual and bodily relaxation at camp. Relieve our tensions, refresh our minds, and strengthen our bodies. Above all, renew and strengthen our faith in You, keep us from sin in our work and play, and send us back to our homes strong and confident in You.

Guide and lead me in all things that I may do nothing to damage the spiritual and physical growth of those for whose welfare I am responsible, and grant that I may leave nothing undone which will serve their welfare. Hear me in the name of Jesus, my Savior. Amen.

For the Missions in Foreign Fields

Gracious God, Father in heaven, You would have all to be saved and come to the knowledge of the truth in Christ Jesus, the Savior. But "how are they to believe in Him of whom they have never heard? And how are they to hear without a preacher? And how can men preach, unless they are sent?"

Make me zealous therefore, dear Lord, to do my part to send preachers of the Gospel to all the world. Since I cannot go personally, make me glad to support with my money the foreign missionary program of my church. Add my prayers and my gifts, heavenly Father, to those of other Christians, and bless their use in keeping workers in the fields which are ready to harvest. Bless the preaching of our missionaries with Your divine benediction that the borders of Christ's kingdom may be enlarged and the earth be filled with the knowledge of Your glory as the waters cover the sea.

Hear my prayer for the sake of Him who died that all might live, even Jesus Christ, my Lord and my Redeemer. Amen.

For Missions at Home

O Lord, You came to seek and to save the lost, give me a heart that yearns like Yours for the souls of lost people. You have earned a perfect salvation for every sinner by Your holy life and bitter death. You have made known the riches of Your grace in the Gospel. You count on me to make Your Gospel known to all nations and have promised to be with me in every mission endeavor.

Keep me from all selfishness, stinginess, and indifference, lest people perish in their sins for want of the Gospel that I have failed to bring them. Give me a love for souls, a liberal and joyful spirit of giving, and a readiness to support the work of missions with fervent eagerness.

Bless the preaching of the Gospel in this my native land. Give the power of Your Holy Spirit to the testimony of our Christian pastors, teachers, and all Your people everywhere. Stir up the hearts of the people of our country so that they will be restless without You and may turn to You to find peace and rest for their souls.

Lord Jesus, You have given me the command to bring Your Gospel to every creature. You have promised to be with me. Give me the grace to be obedient and the readiness to follow You in the search for souls whom You have redeemed with Your blood. Amen.

For Missionary Zeal

Blessed Lord God, who by Your Son commanded me to go into all the world and to preach the Gospel to every creature, increase my faith and zeal that I may more earnestly desire and more diligently seek the salvation of all people. I confess that often my heart is cold and my ears are dull to Your mission cry. I have by no means deserved to be called to Your church and to be privileged to become Your messenger. Forgive my indifference for Jesus' sake, and by Your Holy Spirit fill my heart with a burning zeal to bring the light of the everlasting Gospel to unbelievers both at home and abroad.

Give me a loving heart, sincerity of speech, and piety of life to adorn my Christian profession of faith. May I never by ungodly conduct or unbecoming speech give unbelievers an excuse for criticizing the Gospel of Christ.

Knowing that the day is drawing to a close and that the hands on the clock of time are advancing toward midnight, may I by Your Spirit's prompting support the mission program of my church with my personal witness, my earnest prayers, and my sacrificial gifts. Grant that through me many may be saved from the kingdom of darkness for the kingdom of Your Light, through Jesus Christ, Your Son and our Lord. Amen.

For the Spread of the Gospel
by Radio and Television

Lord Jesus Christ, blessed Savior, how great is Your mercy that You would have all to be saved and come to the knowledge of the truth! Let me always remember Your command to "go into all the world and preach the Gospel to the whole creation that people everywhere may learn to know the truth of Your saving love.

I must confess that I have not always been as active as I might have been in obeying Your command. At times I was even tempted to excuse myself by pleading that there was little that I could do to bring the Gospel to everyone. But now You have given us the marvels of radio and television, by which the story of Your saving love can be quickly carried to all the world. Accept, O Christ, my gratitude and my offerings for these modern ways of going quickly to all the world with Your saving Gospel.

Favor with Your divine blessing the radio and television mission of our church, and by the working of the Holy Spirit make Your Word, carried by the air waves, a power to salvation in the hearts and lives of people everywhere, for whom You died that they might live forever. Amen.

For Ability to Witness

Lord, I thank You for the saving faith and for Your promise of eternal life. Make me ever grateful for these blessings and increase my willingness to serve You, especially to witness of Your gracious love for all sinners.

I pray You, support me with Your power as I witness to others. Too often I have missed opportunities to speak for You. Forgive me where I have failed. Help me to see opportunities for witnessing, and give me the courage to speak up.

Increase my concern for lost souls and my desire to witness, and strengthen me according to need. Lord, I often do not know what to say, but You know; I am often weak and afraid, but You are strong. Make Your love my love; Your words my words; and Your strength my strength. Help me to speak the right word at the right time, and with all Your children on earth help me to go forth to new victories for You; in Jesus' name. Amen.

For the Unconverted

Jesus, Lover of souls, Shepherd of all who stray and make mistakes, You do not desire that any should perish but that all should come to You and find healing from sin, peace of mind, and cleansing from the guilt of conscience. I come beseeching You for my friends who still live without hope in this world and who have closed their hearts and lives to Your gracious invitation to come and find rest and peace for their souls.

Grant me the grace to use every opportunity by word and conduct to bear witness to You and Your love. May all my decisions and interests show my associates that I put You first in my life and thought. May my behavior at all times reveal Your gracious presence in me. Make me thoughtful, considerate, helpful, and patient in their presence. Open the eyes of my companions to see the wonders of Your love, the blessedness of belonging to You, and the joy and satisfaction that service rendered to You gives to me each day. Abide with me, and bless each effort of mine to win souls for You, most adorable Savior and Friend. Amen.

For a Specific Person
to Whom One Desires to Witness

Lord God, who gives all things, I thank You for all spiritual and earthly blessings that have come to me from Your gracious hand. Make me appreciative and useful, and grant that I may always be intent on serving You. Supply my daily needs, and grant that I may receive the gifts of Your goodness with thanksgiving. Help me in all things to put You first, to seek Your glory, and to love and serve my neighbor as myself.

At this time I pray You especially to give me a courageous and wise heart that I may witness of Your love to _____ , who is little interested in the needs of the spirit and his (her) own salvation. Give me the right thoughts to think and the right words to speak, and send Your Holy Spirit into his (her) heart that he (she) may listen and believe. I feel altogether inadequate for the task which is mine to perform, but I know that through You I will be able to do all things. Help me to take courage from the example of the apostles, who trusted in Your promise: "For what you are to say will be given you in that hour; for it is not you who speak, but the Spirit of your father speaking through you."

I depend on You. Lend power and conviction to my halting words, that _____ may find eternal life and joy of salvation in You; through Jesus Christ. Amen.

For the Spiritual Welfare
of Friends, Relatives, and Fellow Workers

Dear heavenly Father, who has so ordered this world that I do not spend my days in lonely solitude but has surrounded me with family, friends, neighbors, acquaintances, and fellow workers, I ask You to look with favor on all whose lives touch mine in the course of my daily activities. Grant them a deep and lasting sense of their sinfulness, and for Jesus' sake lead them to genuine repentance. Give them grace to always seek the forgiveness of their sins and to know the blessedness of those to whom the Lord does not charge their sins. Shield them from temptation by the Evil One. Fill their hearts with the faith that works by love, the hope that does not make ashamed, the charity that never fails, trust in You that shall not be shaken, patience that endures, and courage that shall always confess Christ. May they surrender themselves to Your service and, walking before You in righteousness and holiness all the days of their lives, constantly dwell in Your favor and finally die in Your peace. For Jesus' sake. Amen.

For Opportunities
for Kingdom Service

Dear Father in heaven, I thank You that You have made me a child of Yours and have allowed me to help build Your kingdom. Every day I pray, "Thy kingdom come." With all my heart I want You kingdom to come, and I want to do my part that it may come. Show me how I may help to proclaim Your name and how I may speak of Your glorious majesty and of Your wonderful works.

Open a way of service for me in my congregation. I surrender altogether to Your will. Give me work in which I can serve You best. If it please You, move those who are entrusted with the administration of the congregation to ask me to serve, or give me courage to go to my pastor and to offer my services. Do not let me sit back and wait while I should seek opportunities for service.

Lord, give me the courage to witness for You at home, in my work, on my vacations, or wherever I may be, that people with whom I live and work may know how much I love You. Increase my faith and my love for You, and use my witness for the conversion of unbelievers and for the strengthening of believers. Hear me in the name of Jesus. Amen.

Prayers for the Family Life

My Birthday

Another year of my life has come to a close, and a new day begins for me, Lord God, eternal Caretaker of my life and Lover of my soul in Christ Jesus. You have been good to me through the years. You have given me health and strength, friends and relatives, enjoyments and pleasures, and, above all, Your Gospel with its many promises of peace and forgiveness. My grateful heart praises You.

Give me the grace to dedicate myself to You again on my birthday, and grant me greater willingness to serve You faithfully and continually. Through Your Holy Spirit make me a loyal member of the church, a worthy citizen of the nation, a dutiful member of the household, and a conscientious performer of my work. Let joy fill my heart as I walk in Your ways, performing my duties and meeting my responsibilities with faithfulness every day.

As I receive this new year of grace from Your bountiful hands, may I use each day to glorify You, serve others, and find contentment and peace of mind under whatever conditions I must live. Grant that with Christ in my heart, I may live a fuller and richer life, and finally be received in Your glory, where I shall praise Your mercies and Your goodness forever and ever. Amen.

Upon My Graduation

Dear Lord Jesus, who has been my Teacher and Friend and has shown me that the fear of the Lord is the beginning of wisdom, I thank You for the blessings of the past that have made my graduation possible. Especially do I praise You for the support and prayers of my parents, the patience and devotion of my teachers, and the fellowship and the comradeship of my classmates. You have given me the mental gifts and physical health to achieve the goal I have reached and have blessed my efforts with success.

Forgive me for the opportunities I have neglected, for my failure to do my best in every situation, and for any wrong I have committed during my school life.

Help me to use my talents and improve abilities to Your glory and for the betterment of all people. Continue to teach me Your ways, and give me a deeper understanding of Your good and gracious will. Bless my growth in grace, and enlarge my opportunities for service. Hear me, Lord Jesus, according to Your promise. Amen.

For a Life Companion

Dear heavenly Father, who has said, "It is not good that the man should be alone," I come to You asking for help to find my partner in life. I ask You for guidance, for I am Your child, and You are my loving and heavenly Father. As I seek to assume my place in life and fulfill my mission in this world, I long to share my love with another, to establish a home, and to raise a family. In Your tender mercy lead me to a kind and friendly Christian companion who will appreciate me and return my love. I do not want to be alone, but prefer to share my joys and sorrows with someone I can love—one of my faith and my way of life.

Hear my prayer for the sake of Him who blessed marriage by His presence during His ministry on earth. Amen.

For One Disappointed in Love

Lord Jesus Christ, You are the Lover of my soul and will never leave me nor forsake me. Your tender mercy is from everlasting to everlasting, and Your truth endures to all generations.

You have known the frailty and inconsistency of people. You know how often I myself have betrayed Your love and not respected Your goodness. Forgive me, Lord Jesus, for being lukewarm to Your love, cool to the offers of Your grace, and forgetful of Your sacrifice upon the cross.

Help me to be kind, tenderhearted, and forgiving, even as God, my Father, for Your sake has forgiven me. Remove all bitterness from my heart, and let me show true love to the one who has hurt me.

In my disappointment, give me the grace to be honest with myself and with You. Do not let me become proud and refuse to recognize my own shortcomings. If I have driven human love away by being loveless or unlovable, teach me to return to You for pardon and for the warmth of Your enduring love.

When it pleases You, give me the love of one who will pattern his (her) love after Yours, and then give me the grace to do the same. Amen.

On the Day of Engagement

Dear heavenly Bridegroom, my Lord and Savior Jesus Christ, on this day of my engagement I thank You that You have helped me find a person to love and serve until death shall part us. I pray You, grant that our joy and happiness may remain throughout our lives, and help us always to live not only for ourselves but for You.

O Lord, strengthen us and help our love to mature as time goes on that our engagement and marriage may be a joy to You and to all who know us. When Satan would lead us into quarrels and hatred, help us to know that in so doing Satan is opposing not only us but also You. Make Your strength our strength, and help us to overcome the temptations of the Evil One.

Guide us in Your paths. Keep us pure in thought and action. Make us of one mind in planning our marriage that such planning may help to draw us closer in love. Help our parents to be understanding, and help us to understand them, that together we may look forward to the day of marriage, that nothing in our planning may disturb our happiness.

Make our marriage happy in You, and if it shall please You to give us children, grant that we may receive them as gifts from You and that we may bring them up to love and serve You.

O God, I am so happy that I would like to shout for joy. At all times make my joy a pure and holy joy, and let my greatest joy be that You are mine and I am Yours. Hear me, Lord Jesus. Amen.

On Expecting a Baby
(Mother's Prayer)

Lord, "I praise Thee, for Thou art fearful and wonderful. Wonderful are Thy works! Thou knowest me right well." I am filled with astonishment when I think of Your creation and when I think that You are also using me to take part in the creation of a child. I humbly thank You for the privilege, and I pray You, make of me the kind of mother You want for every child.

Keep me strong and healthy during my pregnancy. Help me to live moderately and wisely, avoiding sin and everything that might be harmful to my unborn child. Give me a cheerful outlook and help both my husband and me to regard the present period as a joyous one. O God, help us even now to prepare for the responsibilities of parenthood, and grant that we may never do anything to harm our child bodily or spiritually.

When the time comes make our present joy complete through the birth of a healthy child, and grant us the grace that we may receive the child as a precious gift from You. Help us always to regard and treat that child as Your blessing.

When the baby is born, give us wisdom to train our child right. May we and our child always be a joy to You and the holy angels, and may we together praise You in all eternity; through Jesus Christ. Amen.

On the Coming of the Baby
(Parent's Prayer)

Lord Jesus Christ, You are the Good Shepherd who delights in small children and gently leads those that are with young, we thank You for Your marvelous mercy. You have granted us the gift of a healthy child, and we cannot praise You enough for

Your loving-kindness. You have guided the physician, given us strength during the pregnancy and delivery, and sustained us until now.

Give us a grateful heart every day of our lives, and let us be the kind of parents who will please You. Keep us conscious at all times of the holy trust placed in us by the gift of this child, and help us to bring our child up in Your fear and favor.

Send Your guardian angels to watch over our little one, and shield him (her) from all danger of body or soul. Bless those who will help us care for our child. Take our child into Your kingdom, and give him (her) an inheritance with all Your saints.

You who have given life to my child, be our Good Shepherd, and lead us in paths pleasing to You. Amen.

For My Wedding Anniversary

Heavenly Father, on our wedding anniversary I come to the throne of grace with a prayer of thanksgiving. I am grateful to You for my spouse. I bless You that by Your direction the pathways of our lives met and our hearts were united in true love.

I thank You, dear Lord, that our love for each other has been preserved and strengthened through the years. In Your divine wisdom good days and bad, health and sickness, and all other experiences have bound our hearts and lives closer to each other and to You, our God and Lord.

I confess that I have not always been as kind and thoughtful as I should have been. I regret that I have sometimes been selfish and indifferent. Help me to make amends. Teach me to be quick to forgive and to forget any fault of my spouse, even as You no longer remember my sins for Jesus' sake.

If it be Your will, grant us additional years of wedded happiness; cause the love that unites us to become stronger each day. When our life is over, take my loved one and me to the heavenly home that You have prepared for those who love You.

I pray in Jesus' name. Amen.

For God-fearing Children

Dear Lord Jesus, who was once a little child, I thank You for the gift of my children. Make me always aware of my responsibility as a Christian parent. You have entrusted to me the bodily and, especially, the spiritual welfare of my children. Bless my efforts to raise them in the discipline and instruction of the Lord.

In Your mercy be near them at all times to guide, protect, support, and comfort them. As in the days of Your ministry when You called the little children to You, even so let my children hear Your kind and beckoning voice through Your Gospel. Make them strong to do Your will. Help them to continue firm in faith in You and in love toward one another. Increase their prayer life. Let their conduct be a shining example that will lead others to know and to love You. Bless them and make them a blessing to all who know them.

Finally, at the end of their lives make them members of Your family in heaven. In Your name I ask it. Amen.

Thanks for Godly Children

Dear God, I thank You for Your countless blessings, especially those of my home and family. You have blessed me marvelously with a Christian spouse and with children who are a joy to me. Accept my humble thanks for the comfort and happiness my spouse and children have brought.

I thank You that You have so graciously blessed the Christian training of my children. You have made them reverent toward You, respectful toward their parents and superiors, and diligent in their work. O God, keep my children in Your fear and favor. When they sin, lead them to repentance and forgive their trespasses. When they rejoice, let them rejoice in You and Your goodness. In sadness, cheer them with Your mercy. In loneliness, comfort them with Your presence.

Make me and my spouse appreciative and sympathetic parents. Help us always to regard our children as Your children. Give us Your grace that we may continue to train them in Your commandments. Give us the wisdom, love, and patience that are necessary to make us good parents. May our trust in You be reflected in the trust of our children. Above all else, bring us and our children into Your everlasting glory; for the sake of Jesus Christ, our Lord and Savior. Amen.

For a High School Son or Daughter

Dear Father in heaven, I commit myself and all members of my family to Your care. You have graciously protected us until today, and I trust Your promise that You will continue to protect and bless us. We need Your presence every hour.

At times I become unduly concerned about my son (daughter) _____ in high school. I know that You have promised to bless the Christian instruction that he (she) has received, and yet I am afraid that he (she) may give in to the temptations of the world. I plead with You, Lord, to go with him (her) at all times. Give the warning from Your Word when needed. Give him (her) the strength to withstand temptation. Keep him (her) always in Your comforting care. Help me to overcome my worries by trusting in You.

Permit my son (daughter) to enjoy their youth in

keeping with Your Commandments. Give him (her) an alert mind to profit from his (her) studies, and prepare him (her) for a useful life. Give him (her) Christian friends who trust in You and who support good character. If it please You, help him (her) find a Christian spouse who will with him (her) walk the narrow way of life.

Lord, my son (daughter) is Yours. I commit him (her) to Your gracious guidance and keeping. Bring him (her) and me and all who are near and dear to me to eternal life; for the sake of Jesus Christ, my Lord. Amen.

For a College Student Away from Home

Lord, I thank You that You have permitted our son (daughter) _____ to grow to adulthood and that You have blessed the Christian instruction and training of his (her) childhood. I pray You, grant that Your Word may continue to be his (her) daily guide and delight.

I pray You also, grant him (her) a realization of the responsibility that goes with a higher education. Help him (her) to view all knowledge in the light of Your Word. Give success to his (her) training for a life of usefulness and service. Bless all useful arts and knowledge, and if it please You, help my son (daughter) have a part in the advancement of knowledge.

Help my son (daughter) always to have true friends and to enjoy a balanced social life. Give him (her) friends that strengthen Christian convictions, and keep him (her) faithful to You and Your Word. Grant that he (she) may find a Christian partner for life if it please You. May Your love in Christ Jesus inspire his (her) love for You and for all people. Help him (her) to remember parents and friends at home, and grant us a joyous reunion in Your own good time.

Hear me in the name of Jesus. Amen.

Of Parents for a Mentally Retarded Child

Lord Jesus Christ, how wondrously You answered the prayer of the woman of Canaan who pleaded with You to heal her afflicted daughter! We come to You, precious Savior, with a prayer for our child, who is mentally retarded. We are anxious to have _____ develop as a normal child. We know that nothing is impossible for Your almighty power. You can heal our child if You will. But we leave everything to Your holy will.

We confess, however that our faith at times becomes weak under the stress and strain of this experience. We do not ask to understand, but pray that You would by Your Spirit strengthen our faith in the promise of Your Word that all things, even our bitterest disappointments, must work together for good to us because You love us and we love You.

We pray You, grant to _____ at least enough understanding that he (she) may learn to know and to love You as the Good Shepherd who gave His life also for him (her) and who will always care for every lamb of His flock.

Hear our prayer for Your name's sake. Amen.

Of Parents for a Physically
Handicapped Child

Lord Jesus, who has said, "Let the children to come to Me, do not hinder them," we brought our child to You in Holy Baptism. By this washing of regeneration You have cleansed _____ from every stain of sin and made him (her) Your very own. We are grateful for this blessing.

But we have another care which we would bring to You. You know, O Lord, that our dear child is physically handicapped. He (she) cannot run and play as other children do. We are troubled, too, about his (her) future. We wonder at times, who will care for our _____ when we are gone.

Forgive us such thoughts of anxious cares, dear Lord! Help us and our child to live day by day, and to cast our cares on You, knowing that You care for us all.

In the meantime give us patience and understanding in caring for _____ . Make this testing of our faith in You be for our and our child's good. We pray in Your name. Amen.

Of Parents for Son or Daughter
Who Has Strayed

Lord God, our heavenly Father, because You yearned for Your children when they went astray, You sent Your only Son to seek and to save the lost. You have a Father's heart and know the anguish we feel over the straying of our child.

Lord, he (she) whom You love is sick in his (her) soul. Recall him (her) from his (her) straying, and restore him (her) once more to the joys of fellowship with You and to the security which comes to those who rest securely in Your fold.

Where we have sinned, forgive us, Lord. If we have been neglectful, unkind, thoughtless, cold, or unreasonable, pardon us and help us to make amends. Preserve us from an unforgiving spirit and a haughty heart in our relationship with our child. Comfort us by Your Spirit, and teach us to rely on You.

For You, O Lord, love our son (daughter) much more than we ever could. You have redeemed him (her), You have called him (her) by name in Holy Baptism. He (she) is Yours.

Deal with him (her) according to the multitude of Your tender mercies, and do not reward him (her) according to his (her) sins. Be gracious to us, good Lord, and reunite us before Your throne of mercy, for Jesus' sake. Amen.

In Marital Difficulties

Lord Jesus, who blessed the marriage at Cana with Your presence, my wife (husband) and I need the sanctifying influence of Your presence in our home. We have not been happy. I confess that we have not always lived our wedded life according to Your Word. We have had differences, ugly scenes, and harsh words. I am ashamed of my conduct, for I, too, have been personally guilty, and I pray You to forgive me my transgressions.

Dear Savior, I pray You, come into our home and live there; then we shall be able to overcome our difficulties. Keep me and my wife (husband) aware of the perfect example of Your unselfish love and service, and make us eager to follow that example in our wedded life. Help us to be willing to forgive and to forget, even as You in Your mercy forgive us our sins and wash them away. Direct me and my spouse to live according to Your Word that every experience may serve to draw us closer to each other and both closer to You. Hear my prayer, blessed Jesus! Amen.

For One Absent from the Family

Dear Father in heaven, I come before Your throne of grace in behalf of _____, who is absent from the family circle. I know You are present everywhere; I know that You also are present where he (she) is now living. But I would pray You today, to let _____ feel Your sustaining presence while in strange surroundings. Protect him (her) when harm and danger threaten body and soul; be close to him (her) in every temptation. Let Your Word be a lamp to his (her) feet and light to his (her) path. Increase his (her) faith and trust in You and in Jesus Christ, our blessed Savior, in whom we have forgiveness of sins.

Though we are far from one another in the body, keep us close to one another in spirit and united by a common faith in You.

At the appointed time grant us a happy reunion with _____ in our family circle, and may every member of our family have a place in the company of the saints in glory everlasting.

Hear my prayer for Jesus' sake. Amen.

For the Families of Those in Service

Lord God of the nations and Ruler of all things visible and invisible, I bring to Your throne of wisdom, grace, and justice the souls of those families who have been separated by the nation's call to service. Help them to adjust to this situation, knowing that You are with each one of them as they are separated one from another.

Preserve them in the faith that saves, and let them learn to lean on You continually. Let none doubt Your protecting care, and grant that they will entrust themselves each day to You and Your almighty hands until they are united again to serve You with one heart and one soul to the end of days through Jesus, our adorable Savior. Amen.

For My Family While I Am in Service

Gracious and good Lord, many perplexing thoughts run through my mind to disturb and irritate me. I know You are acquainted with all my thinking. I and my family are precious to You. I know therefore that You will watch over each member of my family and keep us, one and all, in Your grace. This You have promised to do. Grant that I will not grow cold and indifferent toward You because I am not protected by the family ties at home. Give me the grace to continue to worship You and come to Your throne of grace in prayer as do my loved ones at home. There we meet, Lord God, even though we are miles apart, to pray to You for forgiveness and protection.

Keep our ideals high, our faith strong, and our lives free from sin. Give me and each member of my family the grace to accept with cheerfulness and courage whatever befalls us. Let Your Word be to us a light and guide at all times. Above all, let the day be near when we can be united in our home and together worship and praise You as our heavenly Father in Christ Jesus, who has promised to be with us always, no matter where we are. Hear my requests for Jesus' sake. Amen.

For One of the Family in Service

Lord, You are a God of peace and desire that we should live and let live. You love all people—not only a chosen few. I know You have sent Your Son, my Savior, into the world of sin to bring peace on earth. Yet the wickedness and selfishness of the human race has brought on wars and strife, death and destruction. I beseech You, heavenly Lord, to touch the hearts of the rulers and leaders of the nations with compassion that each may strive to maintain peace among the people of the world.

But, O Lord, I beseech You especially today to protect _____ , who is in the service of our nation. Grant that the faith which is in him (her) from childhood may remain unshaken through the many temptations that beset him (her).

Help him (her) to conquer discouragement, home-
sickness, and doubt. Stand at his (her) side when
tempted to forsake You and to sin. Grant that with
Joseph he (she) will say: "How then can I do this
great wickedness and sin against God?"

As I pray for him (her), remind him (her) to pray
for me. As we are parted by many miles, let our
prayers meet at Your throne of grace. Return him
(her) unstained in character, unshaken in faith, and
ever loyal to You, the eternal Caretaker of our lives,
and faithful to Your Son, Jesus Christ, our Savior
and Guide. Amen.

Family Reunion

Dear heavenly Father, we are gathered here as a
family, some from near, some from far. We thank
You for this privilege of getting together for a few
hours of fellowship, recalling past events, and
honoring loved ones. As we do so, we are reminded
of the blessings You have showered upon us
collectively and individually. Indeed, You have
been good to us, to one and all, to great and small.
Who can count all Your benefits?

We praise You for Your temporal blessings
which are new to us each morning. We thank You
for relatives and friends, health and strength,
prosperity and peace. We also give You grateful
thanks for Your guidance, Your support, and Your

protection both day and night. But, above all, we express our gratitude to You for Your spiritual blessings—for having brought us to the knowledge of Your dear Son, who died for us that we might be His own, to live under Him in His kingdom, and to serve Him in everlasting righteousness, innocence, and blessedness.

May Your Holy Spirit keep us strong in faith, that hereafter we may gather as a family in Your heavenly homeland, where there is no parting and where there are pleasures forevermore.

In Jesus' name we ask it. Amen.

For Travel by Land, Sea, or Air

O Lord, my Guide and Guard, who is present everywhere with Your mighty power, shield me from all danger as I begin my travel. I rejoice with the psalmist: "Whither shall I go from Thy Spirit? Or whither shall I flee from Thy presence? If I ascend to heaven, Thou art there! . . . If I take the wings of the morning and dwell in the uttermost parts of the sea, even there Thy hand shall lead me, and Thy right hand shall hold me."

Give Your holy angels charge over me to keep me in all my ways. Cause them to hold me in their hands, lest I be placed in serious peril.

Give me the common sense to be careful and the Christian judgment to obey those laws designed for my well-being. Keep me from recklessness, lest I tempt You and forfeit the comfort of Your promises to watch over me.

Go with me on my travels. Be my Companion, and lead me safely to my destination. If death awaits me on this trip, keep me in true faith in You that I may reach my destination in heaven, which You have won for me by Your atonement for my sins. Amen.

For Families Having Misunderstandings

1

O Lord, our God, You have said: "Unless the Lord builds the house, those who build it labor in vain." We have forgotten these words, O Lord, and our home is not a joy to You, nor is it satisfying for us. We are not successful because we are not building our homelife according to Your specifications.

Forgive our wrangling and quarreling, our selfishness and pettiness, our suspicions and hatefulness, our lovelessness and unforgiving spirit. Purify our souls by Your Holy Spirit, and enter into our hearts and home with Your pardoning grace.

Help us to be kind one to another, tenderhearted, forgiving one another, even as You for Christ's sake has forgiven us. Turn our hearts and minds to Your sacred Scriptures so that in them we may find the strength through Your Spirit to show love at home. Establish us more firmly in our devotion to You so that we may worship You at our family altar in spirit and in truth.

Bind our hearts together by Christian love, and help us to love one another for the pleasure, happiness, and peace it will restore to us. Amen.

2

Lord, I recognize a happy Christian family life as a gift of Your mercy, and I thank You for every blessing which You have given to me and my loved ones. Now Satan has succeeded in creating jealousies and misunderstandings. We want to do what is right, and we want Your guidance and correction. Do not forsake us in our sorrow, but visit us early with Your mercy, and restore our happiness. Forgive where we have sinned, and guide us back into a family life and love which is pleasing to You.

Help each of us examine ourself to see the causes of the difficulty. Take away pride and selfishness from every heart, and help each of us to say, "Forgive us our debts, as we have forgiven our debtors." Help each of us to see the error of our way and to repent first of all before You. Make each of us humble enough to say: "I have sinned, and I am sorry. Forgive me for the wrong which I have done." Help us all to rejoice again that we are Your children, who trust in You for every blessing of home and family.

Help us to be good examples to one another and to the families we know. Assure us of Your forgiveness. In gratitude to You help us to find peace in anticipation of the glorious harmony that will prevail between us in heaven. In the name of Jesus, our Savior. Amen.

3

Gracious Savior, You have come to life and home to bless those who live under our roof in one household. Enrich our lives with Your presence, and bless us with Your benedictions of grace. I need You, Savior Divine, for we are not getting along as a family. Our misunderstandings are many; daily irritations upset the routine of our household. We get on one another's nerves. Merciful Savior, we need help and guidance and direction. Graciously enter our hearts, and make us, especially me, more selfless and less self-centered. Above all, teach me to realize that each day You are forgiving toward those who have hurt and wounded me. Help me to overcome my petty spirit, my grudges, and my pet peeves. Show me how to appreciate those who are my own flesh and blood, and recognize that they, too, have rights and privileges and deserve consideration. Unite our hearts in Christian love, for Jesus' sake. Amen.

4

Heavenly Father, I am ashamed to confess that we have had a misunderstanding in our family. We have quarreled, ugly words have been spoken, and we are angry with one another. I confess that I, too, have been at fault. I have not paid attention to the gentle advice of Your Holy Word: "So far as it depends upon you, live peaceably with all." In sinning against a member of my family, I have sinned against You.

Forgive me my faults, and help me by Your Spirit to erase from my mind all thoughts of revenge. Make me ready to forgive and forget, even as You in Your mercy forgive and forget my sins for Jesus' sake.

Make all who have had a part in this quarrel in our family eager for reconciliation. Help us to adjust our differences in a manner pleasing to You. May peace and good will and love be restored to the honor of Your holy name. For Jesus' sake. Amen.

Dear Father in heaven, I come before You asking for Your help and blessing. In our family, where there should be peace and harmony and love, there is strife and discord and hatred. I realize that this grieves You, and as a faithful disciple, I want to do all that I can to bring happiness to our family again.

I recognize that I have also sinned. I have not always been as kind and patient and understanding toward the members of my family as I should have been. I am truly sorry for my part in bringing about the discord in our home, and I ask You humbly to forgive these great sins through the merit of Your beloved Son, Jesus Christ.

Help us to be kind one to another, to deal gently with one another's weaknesses, to love You more, and to try to do Your will. Bless our home with Your abiding presence, and restore the peace and happiness we once knew. Fill the hearts of the members of our family with Your love so that we may be more loving in our relations with one another.

Send Him into our home who so frequently graced the home of Mary and Martha in Bethany. In His name we ask it. Amen.

For the Lonely

O Lord, my God, You have said: "I will never fail you nor forsake you." Yet I feel alone. You have assured me that nothing can separate me from Your love in Christ Jesus, my Lord. And yet my heart is distressed by a deadening sense of loneliness.

Lord, to whom shall I go? I believe and am sure that You have the words of eternal life. Strengthen me in my faith, and grant me a greater measure of comfort from Your presence.

Lord, give me the grace in my loneliness to search my soul for its cause. If I am lonely because I have refused to give myself in service to others, forgive me for contributing to my loneliness by my own selfishness. If I am lonely because of loyalty to You and Your Gospel, help me to rejoice in my cross-bearing.

Keep me from all temptations to forget Your watchful presence when I am alone, lest I fall into sin and shame. Direct my thoughts heavenward, bring me into the fellowship of other believers, and use me as a means of bringing joy and blessing to others.

Teach me to pray: "Why are you cast down, O my soul, and why are you disquieted within me? Hope in God; for I shall again praise Him, my help and my God." Amen.

For Parents

Dear Father in heaven, I thank You for having made me a parent. I pray You, help me fully to realize my parental responsibility and the privilege of rearing children for You.

O Lord, You know that, like others, that Christian parents may become fearful when they think of their responsibility to provide for the body and soul of a child and to keep that child on the way of salvation. Forgive me when I become fearful, supply all my needs, and help me to perform my work in child training cheerfully and effectively. Give my children intelligent and responsive minds, and grant that I may always teach them what is right and good. Make them receptive to Your Word; grant them the grace to receive it with joy and to believe in Your saving love.

Give me a calm and even temperament, and help me to lead my children patiently and surely toward physical and emotional maturity. Make them useful and helpful in all things that, young or old, they may be a joy to You and a blessing to Christian people everywhere. Give my husband (wife) and me the grace that we may agree in matters of child training so that together we may lead our children toward heaven and You.

Give our congregation a rich measure of Your grace and the willingness to maintain well-functioning agencies of Christian education as an aid to us in our child-training efforts. May both we and the congregation perform our respective duties joyfully, diligently, and thoroughly, to the glory of Your holy name and to the salvation of souls. In the name of Jesus. Amen.

For Children

Lord Jesus, You were never too busy to pay attention to children, for You dearly loved them. I am happy that You love me and that You have time to listen to my prayers and to answer them.

I thank You that You have made me Your own. As I get bigger and stronger every day, help me to grow stronger in my faith, too.

Bless my parents, whom You have given me, and help me to respect and obey them, to love and treasure them. Forgive me when I disobey them or when I fail to respect them as Your precious gifts. Give them wisdom to train me in the good and the right way, and forgive them when they fail.

Bless my home and every member of my family with a strong faith in You and true love to one another. Teach me to be kind, unselfish, helpful, cheerful, forgiving, and faithful in my duties.

Help me to be like You, Lord Jesus, to grow in wisdom and character and in favor with God and all people. Send Your angels to watch over me, to keep me from all harm of body and soul. Bless me, and make me a blessing to my family and friends. Amen.

Prayers for Various Occupations

Before Going to Work

I thank You, dear Lord, who blesses all honest work, that You have allowed me to see the beginning of another day and have equipped me for the work it brings. Be with me as I leave for work. Help me to face the responsibilities of today with rejoicing.

Remind me that in all things I work for You. Whether I eat or drink, order or obey, plan or execute, let me do it all for Your glory. In fulfilling my duties give me faithfulness to do well the tasks You have set before me. That I may be better prepared for today's demands, hold before my eyes the great work of Jesus by which He redeemed me for You, canceled all faults and shortcomings, and assured me of my place eternally at Your side. May His infinite sacrifice of love prompt me to sacrifice for others.

Give me grace to see in my profession an opportunity for loving service to others. In my associations with them make me quick to forgive, sympathetic to their needs, and joyful in their blessings. Grant this for Jesus' sake. Amen.

On Returning from Work

It is by Your grace alone, dear heavenly Father, that I have completed another day of work for You. I thank You for the health and skills You have granted and for the success You have given to my work.

If I have failed to do my best today, forgive me for the sake of the bitter suffering and death of Your dear Son and my Savior, Jesus Christ. If I have not reflected my Christian faith in my conduct, pardon me, and help me to be a better witness to You tomorrow.

Thanks be to You, Father in heaven, for the protection of today and for a safe return to my home, which You have protected while I was at work.

Grant me renewed strength and vigor for another day of work tomorrow, and bless me with refreshing rest tonight. Enable me to use the earnings from my work to please You and to help others. I ask this in the name of Your Son, who knew the difficulty of work and who shed His blood to earn my relationship with You. Amen.

On Taking a New Position

1

Dear Father in heaven, I recognize work as a

159

blessing from You and also a duty. I want to serve You in my work. I want to provide a comfortable living for myself and my family in keeping with Your word: "If anyone does not provide for his relatives, and especially for his own family, he has disowned the faith and is worse than an unbeliever." I want to support Your kingdom in keeping with Your word: "On the first day of every week each of you is to put something aside and store it up, as he may prosper." And I want to help the poor according to Your word: "Blessed is he who considers the Poor."

To be better able to serve these purposes, Lord, I have taken a new position. Grant that my new work may be enjoyable for me and that I may be able to serve You and others in richer measure through this change of jobs. Whoever You bless is blessed indeed. Therefore I pray You, crown my action with Your gracious benediction. Make me faithful in every duty. Give me a kind and loving heart that I may get along well with my new associates. Give me respect for my superiors, and let me be fair to those whose work I am to direct. In all my actions help me to show that I love You and serve You.

When problems arise in my work, make me patient and persevering until they are solved. When successes come to me, help me to recognize them as coming from You, and keep me humble at all times. Show me how best to use the rewards of my work in serving others and You. Keep me faithful in all things until my earthly work is ended and I shall be in heaven with You; through Jesus Christ. Amen.

2

Lord Jesus, to whom nothing is new or strange, for You know all things, I ask for Your gracious guidance as I assume the responsibilities of my new job.

Grant me the grace to be a faithful steward of the talents entrusted by Your wisdom to my care. Help me to apply myself in such a way that my work will be fruitful and pleasing to You. Give me a sense of honesty and loyalty, and keep me aware of the accounting I must give You for my stewardship.

Above all, give me a true sense of my Christian vocation so that in all things You may be glorified and that all people with whom I come in contact may discover in me the power of Your death and resurrection.

Keep me humble in my successes, cheerful in the face of failure, determined in spite of difficulties, and honest in all my dealings. Bless my work, and use me in my new position to be a blessing to others. Hear me, Lord Jesus, for You are my real Employer, and I am Your servant. Amen.

On Receiving a Promotion

Gracious God, who gives every good and perfect

gift, I come to You with thanksgiving and praise for Your wondrous mercy in granting me this promotion. Help me regard it as a sacred trust from You. Enable me to put my time and talents to the best use. Let me look upon my new assignment not only as a job to be done but as an opportunity for service to others and You.

Keep me conscious of my stewardship, and make me diligent in the performance of my duty. Make me humble and respectful toward those placed over me, cooperative and helpful toward my co-workers, and patient and understanding toward those who report to me. Lead me to perform my duty "not in the way of eyeservice as men-pleasers, but as servants of Christ, doing the will of God from the heart." Teach me in my work to be fair, love mercy, and walk humbly before You, remembering that One is my Master, even Christ, and that all people are my brothers and sisters. And one day allow me to give a good account of my stewardship; through Jesus Christ. Amen.

When Going on Vacation

Lord Jesus Christ, I am grateful for a vacation. I am tired of the routine of daily life. I know that it will be good for me to follow Your example and go "to the other side" for a while, seeking rest and change.

But I would not go without You. I need Your

presence every hour of my vacation. Keep me close to You while I am away from home. Make me strong to resist all temptations to sin and shame. May Your Spirit help me conduct myself as a Christian. Help me to use my vacation wisely that I may be refreshed in body, mind, and spirit.

Send Your holy angels to protect me in my travels. Amid all the dangers of the crowded highways, and wherever else I may be, keep me safe from harm and danger, and at the end of my vacation bring me safely back home again.

In Your holy name I both pray and go. Amen.

On Returning from Vacation

Lord God, heavenly Father, my vacation is over. It was good to be away for a little while from routine everyday life. I am grateful for the relaxation, for the new friends I have made, for the increased appreciation of the wonders of Your world.

Go with me, heavenly Father, on my journey home, and give me a joyful reunion with my loved ones. Grant me the grace to return to my job with renewed enthusiasm, making the most of the talents that You have given me as a sacred trust. Let me find joy in sharing my blessings with those who are less fortunate and in giving cheerfully for the work my church is doing at home and abroad.

Forgive all that was wrong in thought, word, or

163

deed during my vacation, and as I return to my work, help me to walk in the way of Your Commandments. In Jesus' name. Amen.

While on Strike

Dear Father in heaven, I thank You for the blessing of work and of daily bread. Let me never forget Your goodness in providing food and shelter, and grant that I may always look to You for my needs of body and soul.

Because there are disagreements between my labor union and my employer, I am now on strike and out of work. I know You love everyone, and it is Your will that I love all people as brothers and sisters. Therefore help me, my fellow workers, and my employer to overcome all selfishness and pride and to seek a fair solution of our difficulties.

Look with mercy on all who are out of work, and provide for their bodily needs. Give us food, clothing, and shelter, and keep us and our families from suffering and harm.

Protect the property of strikers and employers during the conferences between them. Give our employer a sympathetic understanding of the problems and needs of his workers. Likewise give me and the other workers a proper insight into the problems and resources of our employer, that we may not ask more than is reasonable. Prevent bitterness and strife, and where ungodly strife is present, grant Your healing and peace. Guide the negotiations toward an early agreement whereby both employer and worker may profit. May fairness and justice prevail for all concerned. And when an agreement is reached and we return to work, grant that all bitterness may be forgotten. Help us all to live and work together in unity of heart and mind.

Give Your blessing to honest labor everywhere that the needs of all people may be supplied and that Your kingdom may flourish; through Jesus Christ. Amen.

For the Unemployed

Dear Father in heaven, Giver of all good things, I thank You that You have created me and preserved me to this day. You know my needs and my fears because of my present unemployment. I pray You, comfort and strengthen me, and help me to maintain my hope and courage.

It is clear from Your Word that work is normal and good for all people, yet I have not found the work which I need and seek. This situation is hard to understand. Help me, Lord, to surrender wholly to You and to look to You for the employment that I need.

I pray You, Lord, correct what is wrong with me or with the employment situation in general, and give me the opportunity to earn my living. Open a door to employment which I do not now see. Keep me from discouragement and bitterness, and help me to put my trust in You. Help me to say with a believing heart: "The eyes of all look to Thee, and Thou givest them their food in due season. Thou openest Thy hand, Thou satisfiest the desire of every living thing."

In that knowledge and in that faith make me trusting and patient. In the meantime care for me and mine according to Your promise. I trust You will do so for the sake of Jesus Christ, my Savior, in whom You have promised to give us all things. Amen.

For Business People

Heavenly Father, at the beginning of another day I pray You, teach me to use acceptably the talents that You have entrusted to my care.

Give me a healthy body and mind that I may be able to meet the responsibilities of my position in life. While making money, keep me from the love of money. While gaining the temporal, keep me from losing the eternal.

May I always be honest in my business, not only because honest is the best policy but because it is Your will. Keep me from being covetous and selfish, and let me deal with my employees according to the great commandment, "You shall love your neighbors as youself."

Forgive me where I have failed in the past, and with every passing day let me become a more faithful steward of Your bountiful trust. In Jesus' name I pray. Amen.

For Laboring People

Lord Jesus, You were a carpenter's son and You know the joys and sorrows of a working person. You know the dignity of labor, for You labored by the sweat of Your brow and through Your apostle commanded every person to do "honest work with his hands, so that he may be able to give to those in need." Help me to be faithful in my work, and grant me the grace to work for You, my Master. Enable me to be a source of joy to my earthly employer by giving the best of my service, an honest portion of my time, and a ready willingness to cooperate in carrying out my duties. Give my employer a sense of responsibility to You, and bless the position of trust You have granted to him (her).

Make my work successful so that my earnings can be put to uses pleasing to You. If it is Your will, keep me in good health, and give to me continued employment.

When I fall short of what I ought to be, forgive me, Lord Jesus. Help me in all I do to show that I am Yours and that You are my Lord and Master. Enable me to be a good example by my speech and conduct, so that those with whom I work may be drawn to You and find the joy which is mine in being Yours. Amen.

Labor Leaders

Lord Jesus Christ, who in Your own city of Nazareth worked with Your hands and thus blessed our work. We pray You, look with favor on all skilled and unskilled workers whose efforts supply people with the necessities and comforts of life. In particular, lend wisdom and understanding to me and all those who are labor leaders.

Make me increasingly aware of the importance of my role in conducting the activities of my organization according to Christian principles. Help me to establish and maintain high standards of quality in our crafts. Teach me to be a faithful leader who will direct my group to give unselfish service, as to You, and for the public welfare. Let me bear in mind that we are all members of one great economic body and that the losses of one group adversely affect all the others.

Guide me to work for industrial peace, harmony, and cooperation. Restrain among us all criminal leadership that strives for selfish gain and glory. Fill me with a sense of honor, decency, and responsibility. Impress upon me that one day I must lay aside my tools to appear before Your judgment seat, where I must give an account of my activities. May mine be a good accounting; for Jesus' sake. Amen.

Management

Lord God, heavenly Father, I recognize the responsibility which You have given me in choosing me to be an employer and a manager of people. I know that every success in my work is from You and that my office is a sacred trust that I am to execute for You and for the benefit of all people. I thank You for my position of trust and for every blessing on my work which You have given.

I pray You, Lord, make me adequate for the duties of my office. Give me the mind of Your Son Jesus Christ, who sacrificed that others might gain, who died that others might live, and who always placed the welfare of people above material gain. As I seek to expand business and to increase legitimate profits, keep me honest in all things, and help me to remember that my first service is to You. Make me considerate and kind, and show me how to be fair both to my business and to the people who work for me. Increase my ability to work with people, and give me success in helping them to develop to their full capacity. Grant me the patience to deal with them as a Christian should.

At all times, Lord, keep me true to You and to Your Word, and help me to witness to the fact that You are my Creator, my Redeemer, and my Comforter. Hear me in Jesus' name. Amen.

For Guidance in Vocation

O Lord, heavenly Father, You have promised to watch over Your children wherever they may be and to guide them in all their ways.

Be my Guide in my work, and help me to work in such a way that You will be pleased. Give me the wisdom necessary to make the proper decisions in problems which confront me daily.

Above all else, remind me continually by Your Spirit that You have called me by Your Gospel to be Your child and that it is my business at all times to be a Christian. Grant me a better understanding of my Christian vocation so that all I do in my work may reflect glory upon You, my heavenly Father.

Guide me in paths of integrity and honesty for Your name's sake, lest men mock You because of my denial of You through hypocrisy and dishonesty. Forgive me when I deny You, even as you forgave Peter when he disclaimed You as his Lord.

Help me to use my talents wisely in my work, for I want to give a good account of my stewardship. Enable me to be a blessing to those with whom and for whom I work, to their joy, and to Your glory. Amen.

For Guidance
in the Choice of a Vocation

Dear God, I thank You for a sound body and mind for all my schooling and training. Now the time has come when I must make a choice which will give direction to my life and work. I realize the seriousness of the situation, and I come to You for guidance and counsel.

O Lord, give me the proper attitude toward work. Help me always to remember that it is Your will that I work in a useful vocation, one in which I can serve You and my neighbor. You have given me health and ability. I depend on You to lead me into some work whereby my ability can best be utilized, in which I will be happy and content, and by which I can make a good living. Help me to think clearly, and open the right opportunity for me. If I cannot immediately find the work I prefer, make me patient and persevering, and help me to serve You in whatever work is available.

As I grow in experience and skill, lead me to greater service and responsibility if it pleases You, but keep me always from conflict with others in order to satisfy my own ambitions. I pray You also, show me opportunities to speak for You in my daily contact with fellow workers and give me the faith and courage to confess my faith and to lead others to You. Grant me the grace of a godly life that I may be a witness for You by my daily actions. In all things help me to believe and to do what is right and to be a good worker for You; in the name of Jesus. Amen.

Doctors

Lord God Eternal, Creator of life and Healer of our souls, You have given to us children of humanity a wonderful and useful body, which we are to make temples for You. To me You have granted the privilege to make special study of the human body, its functions as well as its illnesses. Grant that I remember at all times that each patient entrusted to my care is a soul redeemed through Your Son on Calvary and precious in Your sight. Give me the needed wisdom to diagnose each case correctly and to prescribe the necessary remedy to heal the body and to ease its pain. Restore to health and useful living the patients entrusted to my care. I need Your guidance, Your help, O Lord, and the will to meet my responsibilities. Help me to conquer all self-seeking, all irritations, all impatience. Make me cheerful. Help me by my word and action to fill the hearts of my patients with hope, confidence, and courage. Above all, let me realize day after day that

I am dependent on You as my God. May I at all times bear testimony of my faith and my loyalty to Jesus, my Savior and the Great Physician of our souls. Amen.

Nurses

Almighty God, who gives and maintains life, I thank You for having given me the skill and knowledge to relieve suffering and lessen pain. May I always be faithful to my profession.

Give me strength for each day's duties. Make me brave, patient, kind, and understanding. Help me to ease the pain of those entrusted to my care and to bring rest to troubled hearts. In loyal service and devoted care let me reflect Your boundless love.

In my service to the physical needs of others, may I also be granted the privilege of winning souls for You, realizing that people on their sickbed desire not only strength of body but also peace of mind. Let me, O gracious Lord, be one of Your instruments accomplishing Your purposes.

Be near me always to guide me, to help me, and to use me in the ministry to the sick and suffering; for Jesus' sake. Amen.

Workers in Hospitals
and Nursing Homes

Lord Jesus, You are the heavenly Physician who

is able to give health to the body, wholesomeness to the mind, and peace to the soul.

Conduct Your ministry of mercy in all the hospitals and nursing homes of our land, and grant Your healing to the distressed.

Give me patience and wisdom as I minister to the needy, and grant me a special measure of love and understanding toward those who are frightened and in pain.

Walk down the corridors of our hospital, and enter every room with Your tender mercy and healing care. Use me to bring hope and courage to the lonely and the discouraged. Give me opportunities to speak a word for You and Your forgiving grace, and then grant me the grace to speak in a joyful way.

Show Yourself as the Savior especially to the dying, so that at their departing they may inherit the eternal joys and rest of their heavenly home.

Send Your holy angels to watch over us, and grant to all who work here the wisdom each one needs for his (her) appointed task. When I become weary in serving others, keep me from becoming tired of serving. But remind me by Your Spirit that You did not come to be served but to serve, and to give Your life a ransom for many. Hear me, O Lord Jesus, for Your name's sake. Amen.

Lawyers

Heavenly Father, I thank You that You have called me to the honored profession of law, where I have the opportunity to be of special service to You and to all people. Keep me worthy, I pray, of the sacred trust committed to my care.

May I always be aware that the authority of the law has been ordained by You. Help me in the practice of my profession to uphold the laws of our country and of this state. Make me desire to have truth and righteousness prevail at all times. May any counsel I give to those who come to me for advice be in accord with the letter and spirit of our laws and never contrary to Your Word.

If You should grant me success and honor in my profession, I pray You to keep me humble and generous. May my conduct in both my personal and professional life always reflect Your glory. In Jesus' name. Amen.

State Officials

Gracious God, heavenly Father, You have revealed in Your Word that rule and authority in government are in keeping with Your divine order. Keep me mindful, I pray You, of the sacred trust which You have committed to my care by using me, as an officer of the state, to carry out Your plans.

Give me wisdom and understanding that I may

perform the duties of my office for the good of my fellow citizens. Grant me Your grace that I may never use my office to enrich myself nor to serve selfish interests.

Hear my prayer, and lead me in the paths of righteousness in which You would have me walk, for the good of our state and for Your name's sake. In Jesus' name. Amen.

City Officials

Unless You, Lord Omnipotent, keep the city, the wickedness and cunning of sinful people will destroy us. Therefore I come to You, placing in Your hands the needs of our city, asking You to give wisdom and ability, sane judgment, and moral purpose to those who govern us. I know, Lord, that the task if difficult, the duties are many, and the responsibilities heavy. I pray for them that You would support them with Your might, that crime and lawlessness be controlled and righteousness and integrity prevail.

Make me a law-abiding citizen and one who will seek the welfare of the community. Above all, grant that more poeple in our city will accept Jesus as their Savior and serve Him with faithfulness and untiring zeal. Make ours a truly Christian community, and give us officials who will dedicate themselves wholeheartedly to You and to their tasks and assignments. Then Yours is the glory and the praise through endless days. In Jesus' name. Amen.

Teachers

1

Heavenly Father, You have called me to a position of great responsibility as a teacher of growing boys and girls. Keep me aware of my obligation to help prepare them for their place in life and to teach them to be mindful of their duties to God and others.

I pray You, give me patience and kindness, wisdom and understanding, in dealing with the children entrusted to my care. Prevent me from saying and doing anything in the classroom that would offend "one of these little ones."

Help me so to live in our community that both parents and children may see that Jesus Christ lives in me and I in Him.

Bless me and the children today and always. Amen.

2

O Lord Jesus, You are the Teacher sent from God, and You are the Wisdom. To Know You is forgiveness and life and salvation. You are the Truth, and to know You is to know the Father, who did not spare You, but gave You up for us all.

Help me to be a teacher such as You love. Give me the right kind of love for each one of Your children entrusted to my care, that my love will be a true reflection of the love which you have for every individual. Keep me mindful that You have created my pupils and have given them different talents, all of which are intended to glorify You.

Keep me from becoming impatient and fretful. Give me enough success to be encouraged and enough reversals to be kept humble. Enable me to be a loyal co-worker to my associates, and bless their work as well as mine.

Give the parents of my pupils a keen sense of the responsibilities You have given them, and help me to assist them in the training of the young, that in all things You may be glorified.

Grant me the grace to be a godly example of Christian piety, and use me to be a blessing to those under my care. Hear me for Your mercy's sake. Amen.

Technicians

Heavenly Father, You have revealed Your wisdom and glory in the universe and entrusted to us mortals the "dominion" or power "over the fish of the sea and over the birds of the air . . . and over all the earth." What a privilege! What a responsibility, Lord! To me You have opened opportunities and insight into the marvels of Your creation. Grant me the grace to always remember that You are the Creator of all things visible and invisible and that all that I discover, create, and formulate is made possible by Your gracious hand. In Your goodness give me the wisdom and the will to use all my abilities to make the world in which I live a better and more useful world, that all the discoveries and inventions be used for the good of humanity.

Above all, grant that I will always remember that all that I am and all ability I possess comes from You, who has given me more than life, yes, also a soul redeemed through Your Son Jesus Christ. Keep me faithful to Him and steadfast to the church and its saving Gospel. This I ask in His name. Amen.

Scientists

Almighty God, Creator of all, whose glory the heavens declare and whose handiwork the earth reveals, You provided this marvelous world in which I live with definite, unchangeable laws which we can learn and use for our benefit.

I ask You to bless my studies and research to advance the welfare of all people. Keep me from perverting the forces of Your creation to the destruction of humanity. Preserve in me a spirit of dedication to my cause that I may help lead the world to the fullest possible use of the material blessings You have created for its enjoyment. As I work with my instruments and study my test tubes, may I see in all that I do the glories of Your marvelous creation and thereby be led to recognize You as the only true God. Grant that my studies of natural forces may strengthen my faith in the truths of Holy Scripture. Give me the guidance of Your Spirit that I may become more familiar with the revelation that far exceeds the results of scientific research, and may discover the greatest truth ever given to humanity—that Your Son came into this world to redeem and to save sinners. Cause me to accept this truth and to always hold fast to Christ as my personal Savior in a living faith, for His name's and my soul's sake. Amen.

Farmers

Lord God, heavenly Father, the earth is Yours, and the cattle of a thousand hills are Yours. You are the Source of life which created this world with its rich resources.

Help me to be a good caretaker of the land entrusted to my care. Preserve me from forgetting Your ownership and my stewardship, lest I become proud and forget You, or lest I become careless and waste what is Yours. Fill my heart with gratitude for the yield of the land and the fruits of my labors.

If it be Your will, grant me bountiful harvests so that I may joyfully praise You and bountifully share these blessings for the spreading of Your saving Gospel. Grant rain in due season, and bless us with good weather. Prevent any disease and disorder that may destroy what You have created. If You see fit to afflict me with failure, keep me humble and penitent, and guard me against complaining and dishonoring You.

I thank You for Your past blessings on my labor. Without You I can do nothing. In everything You must give the increase. You have been good and gracious, heavenly Father, and I ask You, for Jesus' sake, to continue to be merciful to me and to bless me. Amen.

Of a Handicapped Child of God

Heavenly Father, You are the Refuge and Strength of all who put their trust in You. You are a very present Help in trouble, and You supply grace for every time of need.

Teach me by Your Holy Spirit to glory in my infirmities and to discover the meaning of Your gracious promise: "My grace is sufficient for you, for My power is made perfect in weakness." Help me to discover Your strength when I am weak, that I may with fullness of heart praise You for Your mighty care.

When I am tempted to moodiness and despair because of my handicap, when the devil taunts me and tells me that You do not love me, when others are thoughtless and unsympathetic, give me, dear Father in heaven, a clear vision of the Cross of Your dear Son. Show me the bitterness of His suffering in my behalf, the agony of His crucifixion endured for my redemption, and the power of His resurrection for my deliverance from sin and death and hell.

Show me the advantages of my handicap and the blessings which are mine because of it. Especially do I praise You for the kindness of my loved ones, the thoughtfulness of my friends, and the opportunities I have to reflect the love which You have shown me in Christ Jesus, my Lord. Amen.

Prayers Pertaining to National
and International Life

For Peace

Almighty God, Lord of harmony and peace, who sets the limits and boundaries of the nations and marks the paths of history in Your wisdom, justice, and goodness, cause all strife and misunderstanding to cease, and grant peace to our nation. We all are the children of Your creation and of Your love, and You have sent Christ Jesus to this world of sin and wickedness to redeem each one of us living on the earth. You have offered to all of us the Gospel of forgiveness and reconciling peace through the precious blood of Your dear Son.

Grant all of us the grace to accept Your terms of reconciliation, and let me, too, enjoy the forgiveness of all my sin. I ask You, because of Your pardon to us, to make us forgiving, thoughtful, and considerate of one another. Grant that we of this generation may live side by side in quietness and peace, recognizing that each one of us has rights and privileges given us by You in Your goodness of heart. Teach me to look on others as fellow redeemed and permit them to enjoy those blessings that I want as my own.

Make our nation a righteous nation and us

citizens a law-abiding and moral people. Grant health and strength and wisdom to those in authority, especially to our President, and prevent godless and wicked people from corrupting our land. From day to day grant me the grace to live peaceably with those in my community, at work, at the church, and with the associates of my leisure hours, that my conduct and speech may give honor to You and Your Son Jesus Christ, my Savior. Amen.

For Government

Almighty God, our Help in ages past, our Hope for years to come, of whom is all rule and authority in the world, I come before You with a prayer for our government. I am grateful for the good government that You have ordained to rule in our land. You have blessed our country and our people. Bless, I pray You, all who are in authority in our land with wisdom and understanding, with love for righteousness and peace, that under their leadership our country may continue to enjoy Your grace and favor.

Help me, by Your Spirit, as a good citizen to give our government the things which belong to the government and not to forget that I must give You my God, what belongs to You. May Your name be hallowed! For Jesus' sake. Amen.

For the President of
the United States

Almighty God, Ruler of the nations, regard with favor Your servant, the President of the United States. Grant him (her) health of body and mind; make him (her) strong to bear the burdens of his (her) high office. Give him (her) wisdom and understanding, that under his (her) leadership our nation may be directed in the ways of righteousness and peace.

Teach me and all Christian citizens to realize that rule and authority in our country come from You and that our President is Your minister in the administration of his (her) office. Keep us mindful of our obligation to support our President with fervent prayer and ready obedience to the laws of our country.

Bless our President, I pray You, and make him (her) a blessing to our people, to the glory of Your holy name. For Jesus' sake. Amen.

For the Nation

Heavenly Father, Ruler of nations, I thank You for the countless undeserved blessings that You have showered on our country. Individually and as a nation we have sinned often and grievously, and I pray You, mercifully forgive our many sins. Endow the leaders of our country with wisdom from on high. Cause them to rule in Your fear and according to Your will, that we may lead a quiet and peaceable life in all godliness and honesty and that our nation and its people may prosper both spiritually and temporally.

Hold Your protecting hand over our nation, over me and mine, and over all Your children. Preserve our priceless religious liberty, and keep all believers faithful to You. Bring a great salvation to pass, and turn the hearts of multitudes of unbelievers to accept the peace and comfort that only faith in their Savior Jesus Christ can bring them.

Give us faith instead of unbelief, courage instead of fear, love instead of hate, peace instead of quarrels and war, and righteousness instead of sin everywhere and in everything. We have indeed deserved nothing but punishment for our sins, but in Your great mercy be gracious to us, bless us, and hear our prayer for Jesus' sake. Amen.

For the City

O Lord, our God, who is a God of order and justice and is pleased when people govern and are governed according to Your will, I ask You, in the name of Jesus Christ, to bless this city and its inhabitants.

Bestow Your guidance upon all who are in authority. Keep them mindful of their sacred trust in public office, and grant them wisdom for their difficult tasks. Give them a sense of honesty and decency, a spirit of humility and service, and a sensitivity to the needs of every citizen.

Give to all who live here a grateful heart for the advantages we enjoy, ready obedience to our laws, and a profound concern for the rights and privileges of every citizen. Help me to be a light of the world and a salt of the earth in my community, and a blessing to my neighbors.

Protect our city from all calamities and epidemics, and shield us especially from those temptations which could corrupt our officials and cause our citizens to despise You, who is Ruler of all.

Bless the preaching of Your Gospel in our community so that more who live in our city may find their way to the eternal city which has foundations, whose Builder You are and which You have prepared for them that love You. Amen.

For Friendship Among the Nations

O Father of all people, who at the birth of Your Son sent Your holy angels to proclaim good will to all people, foster and promote friendship among the nations of the earth. Impress on people everywhere, regardless of color, race, or national origin, that they are the children of Your creation, and keep them mindful of their common humanity.

Preside in the councils of world leaders to adjust in friendly fashion all differences that separate nations. Let the love that prompted Your Son to give His life for our redemption take root in the hearts of those who are charged with the direction of national affairs. Make them realize that they owe a responsibility not only to their own people but also—and above all—to You as the Ruler of nations to conduct international relations peaceably as much as lies within their power, for the common welfare.

Bless all efforts to promote friendship and understanding among nations. Enable people everywhere to remove from their thoughts and actions every trace of national pride and selfishness and to extend the hand of welcome and fellowship to foreigners. Cause us to recognize our own faults and shortcomings, and establish Your will among the nations of the earth. Bring this to pass, we pray, for Jesus' sake. Amen.

For Better Understanding Among the Nations

O Father of all people and Ruler of nations, who would have all people to dwell together in peace and unity, raise up, we ask You, leaders in every land who will choose peace instead of war and direct their people in pathways of friendship and under-standing toward others.

Help us all in our respective places to seek justice, to cultivate righteousness, and to walk humbly before You. Remove all pride from our hearts. Give us understanding minds so that, regardless of race or nationality, color or station in life, we may realize that we are all of the same flesh and blood, Your common creation.

Restrain the efforts of those who would sow seeds of hatred and ill will among nations. Bless all efforts for peace. Direct the course of this world that Your will may be done and Your kingdom come. Cause quiet and order to prevail everywhere, that the message of Your Gospel may without any obstacle or hindrance be carried to the far corners of the earth; for the sake of Him who died and rose again that we might live forever. Amen.

For Washington's Birthday

Almighty God, Lord of the nations, today we commemorate the birthday of the man we honor as the first President of our country. I thank and praise You for the God-fearing citizens who served our nation in those critical early days. I thank You especially for the wise leadership of George Washington; I am grateful for the inspiration of his confession that "no people can be bound to acknowledge and adore the Invisible Hand which conducts the affairs of men more than those of the United States."

While I am grateful today for all that George Washington and other great presidents have done for the good of our country, I want to acknowledge that it was Your goodness, O God, that has made and kept us a great nation these many years. Teach me and my fellow citizens to remember that "Unless the Lord builds the house, those who build it labor in vain." Forbid that the Christian people of our country should ever forget You, lest we lose Your favor. In Jesus' name. Amen.

For Memorial Day

Almighty and eternal God, Ruler of individuals and of nations, I bring my thanks to You this Memorial Day for all the blessings that You have given our nation. Prosperity has reigned in our country, and enemies have not been able to subdue us, because You have graciously held Your protecting hand over us. Help me to know and to acknowledge that freedom, prosperity, and other blessings come from You, and make me thankful.

I confess, Lord, that Your blessings are entirely undeserved. Irreverence, lust, theft, murder, and sins and crimes of every description are the shame of our privileged country, and with others I can only bow before You in shame. Merciful Father, forgive our personal sins and our national sins for Jesus' sake. Enlighten us by Your Word. Make us upright citizens of our dear country and worthy members of the community in which we live. Move us to bow under authority, first under Yours, and then under the authority of our government. Give us and all the countries of the world a lasting peace, and teach us to live together as befits Your children. Bring about a mighty Christian revival, and turn to You the hearts of millions who now live in unbelief.

As my memories go back to those who have died to preserve our liberties, make me grateful and humble. Give me the determination to do all in my power to safeguard our freedom. Make me diligent in prayer for my country, guide and lead those in authority with Your sure counsel, and give power to all Christian witness that not only the Christians of today but also many others may be brought to eternal life through You; for Jesus' sake. Amen.

For Dominion Day

Lord of the nations, who sets the limit to the powers of humanity and allows nations to run their appointed course, on this Dominion Day I praise You, most holy God, that You have established and preserved this Dominion in the free world of our day. Ours has been a glorious liberty and ours a wonderful country to live in, a vast and prosperous homeland extending from the Atlantic to the Pacific and to the regions of the frozen North.

I beseech You, Lord of heaven and earth, protect us from war and disaster, from sorrow and tears, from atomic destruction. Give us wise leaders, unselfish servants, who at all times place the welfare of the people first. Continue to let us live at peace with the United States and show the nations of the world that two great governments can live side by side without fear, suspicion, and envy and without border fortifications. Preserve this splendid and friendly relationship and good will between us.

On this day, then, accept my thanks as I make known my appreciation to all for the privilege of being permitted to live in this good and blessed land. Continue to be with us as You have been in the past, through Jesus Christ, my Savior and Lord. Amen.

For Independence Day

O God, our help in ages past, our Hope for years to come, I give You grateful thanks on this anniversary of the signing of the Declaration of Independence for the priceless blessings of liberty that with Your help were won for me by my ancestors. Stir up within me, I pray You, a new appreciation of the life, liberty, and pursuit of happiness I enjoy in this land of the free, and a greater readiness to serve my nation with my talents. Teach me, above all, to treasure that precious freedom of conscience and worship, without which other liberties would not long survive. May I never contribute to the loss of these dearly won blessings by my own selfishness, ambition, or indifference.

Teach me furthermore, O Lord, that the enjoyment of freedom brings with it the responsibility to serve. To that end make me willing to respect the laws of my country, to serve my fellow citizens well in any office of trust to which I may be elected, to exercise faithfully my privilege to vote, and to give my loyal support to all public institutions.

Bless all those in authority. Give wisdom and faithfulness to those in positions of leadership. Preserve them from becoming the prey of selfish pressure groups, and give them willingness to serve the interests of the public.

Grant enduring peace to our country and its institutions, so that Your Gospel may be able without hindrance to turn the hearts of all from the bondage of sin to the freedom won by the blood of our precious Redeemer, in whose name and for whose sake we ask this. Amen.

For Labor Day

Lord Jesus, who as a youth worked in Joseph's

carpenter shop, making Yourself useful, help me to perform my work with faithfulness and a cheerful heart. Bless management and labor. May all who must work together in office and shop be mindful of the Golden Rule that You have given to all people, and, following Your directions, give the best possible service one to another. May we all seek each other's good, be thoughtful, helpful, and courteous.

Prosper the nation, that all may find employment and none suffer from want. Give to us who have much the grace to share with those who are unable to work because of sickness and weakness of body. Above all, grant that all people of the world, burdened with sin, may come to You and Your Cross to find healing and salvation. I ask this of You, my Savior and my Lord, who has come into the world to seek and to save those who are lost. Amen.

For Veterans' Day

Lord Jesus, the Captain of my soul, who endured the pain of battle with the old evil Foe in order to secure my redemption, grant me a grateful heart for the freedoms I enjoy through Your grace and mercy.

Help me to treasure my spiritual freedom from sin, death, and the devil, and open my lips continually to praise You for my liberty in You.

Teach me to be thankful for my liberties in this blessed land, which were won and preserved for me by the sacrifices of my countrymen. Help me to honor their memory by a conscientious and loyal citizenship and a readiness to defend the rights of free people everywhere.

Grant Thy comfort to families who today remember with sorrow the death of one who gave his (her) life for our country. Sustain those veterans who are confined to hospitals throughout our land, who bear the scars of war, so that I might enjoy the wholesomeness of peace and freedom.

Keep me from forgetting the heroes of the past, lest I become a coward in the face of the future. Grant the gift of peace to our land and to the world, so that Your Gospel may have free course and more people everywhere may march under Your lordship beneath the banner of Your Cross. Amen.

For the Opening of Congress

At the opening of a new session of Congress, I pray You, heavenly Father, to take into Your gracious care all members of the Senate and of the House of Representatives, the presiding officers, and all other officials. Endow them with a high sense of responsibility of the office to which they have been elected. Make them immune to the temptations of selfish interests. Fill them with knowledge and wisdom, that the resolutions adopted and the laws enacted may meet Your standards and be for the good of our people.

Keep me and my fellow citizens from unfair criticism and faultfinding. Help us rather, O God, at the opening of this new session to render to the members of Congress the honor and respect that is proper and to support them with our prayers and our good will.

Bless our country, bless our government, bless our people, and make our nation a blessing to the people of the world. For Jesus' sake. Amen.

During Wartime

Lord Jesus Christ, Prince of Peace, You hate wars, where people kill their own brothers and sisters and destroy those things that You have given us to enjoy. Forgive us for wars and fightings among us and for the lust of our flesh that breeds them.

O Lord, who makes wars to cease, bring a speedy end to this reign of destruction and terror. Restore all people to sanity so that they may see the insanity of war and avoid it as an instrument of evil and an offense to Your holy majesty.

Turn the hearts of our enemies to peace, and crush in Your power all those who would destroy the creatures You have made to honor You.

Plow deep into the souls of people everywhere, that the precious seed of Your Gospel may take root and bear the fruits of faith and love, that the whole human race may find peace in You.

Keep me in the true faith, that whether I live or I die I may be Yours and You may be mine to adore and to praise forever as the Lamb slain for my sins from before the foundation of the world.

Abide with me, Lord Jesus, that I may ever abide in You and forever with You. Amen.

By Men and Women in the Armed Services

Merciful Father in heaven, I thank You for Your presence and for the comforting assurance of Your love and guidance; for the salvation in Jesus Christ; for the consolation of Your Word; for my praying relatives and friends both near and far; for Your protection in danger and temptation.

Lord, I pray You, go with me day by day and from job to job. Forgive my sins for Jesus' sake, and strengthen my faith. Help me to serve my country ably and loyally, and, above all, keep me faithful to my Lord and Savior Jesus Christ. Keep me loyal also to relatives and friends, and keep them in Your loving care until I return to them. Strengthen me in the conviction that my service in the Armed Forces is a service to my country and to You. Help me to overcome every sin and temptation, and give me the necessary strength for a holy, reverent, chaste, and honest life in word and deed.

Make me an example to my fellow Christians and to unbelievers alike. Give me the courage to confess Your holy name and to witness for You as I have opportunity. Strengthen my love for the whole cause of the Christian church, and help me to work and to sacrifice that Your name may be glorified. Grant graciously that my whole life may be a service to You; in the name of Jesus Christ. Amen.

During Unfavorable Weather

Lord God, who gives rain and sunshine, summer and winter, cold and heat in due season, we ask You in these days of unfavorable weather to uphold us and provide for the needs of all Your living creatures. As Your chastening hand tries our patience and tests our faith and reliance on You, we ask You to forgive our many sins of ingratitude. So often have we forgotten to thank You for Your goodness and acknowledge Your many mercies. We confess that we have not at all times sought You to bless us and our daily work. Forgive us and teach us to look up to You each day, appreciative of rain and sunshine, warmth and cold, planting and harvest, as You in Your wisdom through all kinds of weather conditions do feed us all.

In Your mercy give us weather that is favorable to our needs as a nation and people. Protect us against storms and cold, against hunger and want. Pour out Your blessings and benedictions on us, and make us grateful and thankful for all that we receive from Your bountiful hand. Then Yours shall be the praise and the glory through Jesus, Your Son and our Redeemer and Friend. Amen.

For Rain

Almighty God, who controls the wind and the waves, we come to You asking for rain. At such a time as this we realize particularly that we are small and sinful and that You are great and good. But You have promised to take care of Your children, and we know that Your promises are sure. Therefore, through the atoning death of our blessed Savior, which has made us Your beloved children, we are confident in bringing our present request to You. O Lord of all, open the windows of heaven and send Your showers of blessing.

We have prepared the soil and have planted the seed. But if You do not send sunshine and rain, all our efforts are in vain. Be pleased, therefore, to hear our petitions, and send us refreshing rain, that the parched land may be moistened and the thirst of Your creatures quenched.

O Lord, who satisifies the desire of every living

thing, we praise and glorify Your name and proclaim Your goodness to all people. Grant our
request, if it be Your will, for Jesus' sake. Amen.

In Days of Drought

God of mercy and faith, we come to You
chastened and penitent, and we pray You, do not
look on our sins, and do not punish us in Your
displeasure. The heat and the drought have taken
their toll; the fruits of the field languish for lack of
rain. Many hearts are weary and fearful. We know
we have deserved none of the good things that You
have given us, and we do not deserve an answer to
our prayers. But in Your mercy You have promised
to send the early and late rains and to water the
earth that it may bring forth fruit in due season.
We appeal to Your mercy and to Your promise.

Refresh the drooping fields with rain as in the
days of Elijah. Spare the beautiful trees of Your
creation, revive the grass and the flowers, and help
us to regard them all as gifts of Your love and as
evidences of Your gracious, almighty power. Give
us and all Your creatures the food that we need.
Help those who have been impoverished by the
drought. Open the hearts of the fortunate toward
the unfortunate. Remind us that we depend on
You, and draw us and all people closer together in
peace and in good works.

Help us to walk in Your commandments and to turn to You in every need. Refresh and renew our bodies and minds that we may rejoice in You. In prosperity or adversity help us to sing praises to You; for the sake of Jesus Christ, our Lord and Savior. Amen.

Prayers in Time of Sickness

Before an Operation

As I face this operation, gracious Father in Christ, I come to You with my fears and misgivings and ask You to put in my heart the needed courage to face the day with confidence because of Your goodness and protection. You do not slumber nor sleep while I am in a deep sleep. Let this be an assurance to me that I need not worry or be afraid. Relax my nerves, put my mind at ease, and graciously forgive me all my sins.

Give the surgeon a steady hand and the necessary understanding to do his (her) task with ease and perfection. Give my family the reassuring faith that You are with us, the Keeper of my body and the Lover of my soul. Calm their troubled spirit during the coming hours of my operation. In Your precious hands I put my well-being for time and eternity. This I ask in the name of my Lord and Savior Jesus Christ. Amen.

After an Operation

My grateful heart praises You, heavenly Father, that You have safely seen me through this operation. I know all went well because You watched over me. During the hours and the days which lie ahead ease my distress and pain, and heal me. Give me the needed patience, the necessary endurance, and continued confidence that Your goodness and love will uphold me.

Grant that all service which the nurses give to me will speed my recovery, and then bring me safely home, completely healed. Give me restful days, and bless me tonight with refreshing sleep. Let me enjoy Your peace through the forgiveness of all my sin, for which Christ paid in full on the cross. Continue to abide with me now and always. Amen.

Prayers for the Sickroom

1

Lord Jesus Christ, You were never too busy to spend time with the sick and those afflicted with pain. I ask You to continue to show mercy to me in my illness and to comfort me with Your presence.

Give me a repentant faith in You, for my illness reminds me that I have sinned against You. Wash my sins away in Your blood, and strengthen my faith in Your promises of perfect pardon.

Sustain me in my moments of discouragement. Grant relief from my pain if it will be for my good. Bless those who wait on me, and help me to make their task lighter by cheerfully appreciating their kindness.

Grant healing in Your good time, O Lord. Bless me with patience, and help me to wait on You for a release from my sickness. Keep me from complaining. Watch over the loved ones from whom I am separated, and preserve them in true faith and good health.

I wait on You, Lord Jesus, and in Your Word do I hope. Amen.

2

O Lord Christ, who is the Physician of bodies and souls of all people, who forgives all our sins and heals our diseases, I ask You to step into my sickroom and deal with me according to Your wisdom and mercy.

Help me to see myself as I really am, a sinner deserving Your wrath and punishment, yet Your disciple and heir of Your forgiveness and salvation. Keep on reminding me by Your Spirit of Your great love for me, for I am plagued frequently by disturbing doubts and fears. Remove from me the worries concerning the expenses caused by my sickness and the discomfort I am causing others by my illness. Reassure me that You will provide for all my needs according to the riches of Your grace.

Keep me from feeling sorry for myself, but give me instead true sorrow over my sin and a lively and persevering hope in Your mercy. Grant me the grace to be grateful to those who wait on me and demonstrate their love for me through their service. Restore me to health, if it be Your will, when it is Your will. I commit myself, my body and soul, into Your keeping.

I trust You, Lord Jesus, and I know I can rely on You to do what is best for me. Amen.

3

Almighty God, Author of life and health, I come before You asking that You would help me in my bodily need. In Your wisdom You have laid me on this bed of illness and pain. Be merciful to me, O Lord, and, if it be Your will, give me relief from my suffering. Bless the efforts of my doctor to restore me to health. Grant me steady improvement until I am entirely well again. Preserve me from relapses or complications, and make my recovery swift and complete.

Meanwhile give me patience to await Your deliverance. And if it should be Your will that I linger on my sickbed, grant me the confidence that You do all things well. When Your will is accomplished in me, deliver me from this cross that You have laid on me.

Through this experience draw me closer to You. Watch over my bed. Preserve me from temptation by the Evil One. Grant me the courage to look into the future unafraid, knowing that You are with me and that I have no cause to fear.

Help me by this experience to grow more Christ-like in my attitudes, and finally by Your mercy bring me to everlasting glory. Grant this for Jesus' sake. Amen.

4

Dear heavenly Father, in my weakness I come to You asking for help. I need You so much, and I realize how helpless I am without You. I ask You to give me strength for today, and I will not worry about tomorrow.

My physical illness reminds me of my spiritual illness. You are also the Physician of my soul. Grant me the peace of mind that comes from sins forgiven and the joy of knowing You as that Friend who is closer than a brother or sister.

If I recover from this illness, help me to serve others and to glorify You. Keep before me the blessed example of Your beloved Son, who went about doing good.

Make me patient and grateful. Bless the doctors, the nurses, and all who are taking care of me. Watch over my loved ones while I am absent from them.

Stay close beside me always, and finally take me home to You in heaven. In Jesus' name I ask this. Amen.

5

I thank You, gracious God, for Your comforting word, "Call upon Me in the day of trouble; I will deliver You and you shall glorify Me." I confess that I am unworthy to appear in Your presence, for I have sinned much and have indeed deserved nothing but punishment. But You are a gracious God who, for the sake of Jesus Christ, has forgiven me my sins and remembers them no more.

So I accept Your invitation to call upon You in this day of trouble; I pray You to deliver me from the sickness of my body. I would not tell You how and when to make me well, for You know what is best for me.

Answer my prayer, dear Lord, by sending me that deliverance which is in keeping with Your gracious plans for my life. I promise to glorify You with all that I am and have. In Jesus' precious name. Amen.

6

Lord Jesus Christ, who is the Savior of my soul, I pray You, be the Savior also of my body. If it be Your will, make me well again. I know that Your miracle-working power is not shortened and that You can heal my sick body even though all earthly helpers should fail. As You left everything to the will of Your heavenly Father in Gethsemane, so I leave everything to You; for Your will, not mine, is best.

Bless those who wait on me during my illness, the doctors, the nurses, and all others. Bless those who are praying for me. Reward them all according to Your loving-kindness. Hear my prayer, Lord Jesus. Amen.

7

Divine and gracious Savior, I ask You to take full possession of my heart and life. Let me know that each moment of today You are with me, protecting me with Your grace and preserving me through Your love. Help me to overcome the discouragements that are coming to me and ease my pain. Remove from my heart all self-pity, take all resentment from my mind, and let me live trustingly one day at a time as I lean on You. Give me a hopeful outlook for today, and remove all irritation from the coming night. Let my patience increase as I consider Your mercies, precious Savior. Amen.

8

I lift up my eyes to You, O Lord, my Refuge and

Strength. Trusting in Your promises, I know that You will not fail me in this hour of trouble and that You will give me the strength I need and the help that is necessary. Today let Your mercies again override all my worries. Keep me calm, untroubled, unalarmed. Ease my pain, and let Your divine forgiveness speak peace to my soul through Jesus Christ, my Lord. Fill me with cheerfulness and patience, hope and confidence.

Bless our household with a greater faith and a larger hopefulness as we carry on from day to day in this trouble and in my illness. Remove from my heart all fears and misgivings. Give me a quiet and restful day and a peaceful night of sleep. I ask this in Jesus' name. Amen.

9

Heavenly and gracious Father in Christ Jesus, as I come to Your throne of grace and mercy, fulfill Your promise to be with me and to deliver me out of all my distresses and pain. I need encouragement and strength, which can come only from Your almighty hand. Enable me to entrust myself completely to Your care, giving me hope and patience, courage and confidence.

In Your loving-kindness forgive me all my sin. Put my mind completely at ease because I know that I have You as heavenly Father, and relax my nerves because I can rely on You to watch over me every hour of the day. Bless those who take care of me, and let Your healing hand bring about a speedy recovery.

Purify my heart, uplift me by Your Spirit, and let me live trustingly in Your presence. Let the continued blessings of my Savior comfort me as I remember that through Him I am a child of Your household and coheir of life eternal. Give me a quiet day, and bless me tonight with refreshing sleep as I receive Your benediction through Jesus Christ, the Shepherd of my soul and the closest Friend of my life. Amen.

10

"Save me, O God! For the waters have come up to my neck. I sink in deep mire, where there is no foothold; I have come into deep waters, and the flood sweeps over me. I am weary with my crying; my throat is parched. My eyes grow dim with waiting for my God. . . . O God, Thou knowest my folly; the wrongs I have done are not hidden from Thee. . . . But as for me, my prayer is to Thee, O Lord. At an acceptable time, O God, in the abundance of Thy steadfast love answer me. . . . Answer me, O Lord, for Thy steadfast love is good; according to Thy abundant mercy, turn to me. Hide not Thy face from Thy servant; for I am in distress, make haste to answer me. Draw near to me, redeem me." Amen. (Selected from Psalm 69.)

11

Lord Jesus, Strength of the weary and a very present Help to all who are in distress, I come to You with all my burdens and sins. Send Your divine cleansing and healing into my life. Safely see me through the troubles and pains of the day. Take all sinful thoughts and worries out of my heart, and let me find peace in You. Lead me daily to Calvary to behold Your boundless love, O gracious Savior.

Fill my soul with the joy of forgiveness and the hope of everlasting life. Let not the sufferings and the cares of today make me despondent, but teach me to believe that Your abiding presence will uphold me from hour to hour and from day to day. Keep me from worrying about tomorrow, remembering that "the day's own trouble [is] sufficient for the day."

Give me peaceful days and restful nights. Bless me with sleep. Grant me health in body, soul, and mind. Comfort my soul with the promises of Your word, and keep me steadfast in the faith to the end. Make me grateful to those who are caring for me. Bless this household, and keep all of us cheerful, hopeful, and confident, trusting in You to do all things well. I ask this of You, who has redeemed me with Your own blood. Amen.

Prayers During the Convalescent Period

1

Gracious Father in heaven, Your hand has been heavy on me, and the days of my illness have been trying. I thank You for the chastening, for through it You have drawn me closer to You, and through it I have learned more than ever to realize that You are my loving Father. I pray You, forgive my fears and impatience during my severe trial, and forgive also the bad moments that I have caused those who lovingly cared for me. Remember no more any ingratitude that I may have shown.

I am now on the road to recovery. Lord, help me to praise You every day and to remember Your goodness and mercy. In the pain and difficult moments which still lie ahead, help me to think of the sufferings of Jesus Christ for my salvation; when I become impatient, help me to think of Your patience with sinful people; when I fear for my salvation, help me to remember that my faith is preserved by the power of the Holy Spirit and not by anything that I can do.

Make me humbly grateful for every blessing that You have given. Make the time of my convalescence pass quickly, and restore me to useful service if it please You to do so. Open ways for me to show my gratitude to You and to those who have served me in my illness, and finally bring me and all who are near and dear to me into Your glorious presence, where sickness and sorrow will be no more; through Jesus Christ. Amen.

2

Heavenly Father, by Your goodness I am recovering from serious illness. I was very close to death but You have mercifully answered the prayers that were made for my recovery. I am indebted to You for the healing of my sick body.

"Bless the Lord, O my soul; and all that is within me, bless His holy name! Bless the Lord, O my soul, and forget not all His benefits, who forgives all your iniquity, who heals all your diseases, who redeems your life from the Pit, who crowns you with steadfast love and mercy!"

For the period of convalescence grant me the grace to resign myself to Your holy will. Help me to be patient when complete recovery is slow in coming. Open my eyes to see how You make all things, even my sickness and weakness, work together for my good. May Your peace, which is greater than all human understanding, fill my heart and mind. In Jesus' glorious name. Amen.

3

Heavenly Father, You have told Your children to pray confidently in the name of Your dear Son. You have assured all that trust in You that You never grow tired of the pleas of Your children or turn a deaf ear to their prayers.

Because You have invited me to Your throne of grace, I ask You, if it be Your will, to continue to bless my recovery and to restore me to healthful and helpful activity once more. Thank You for having favored me with healing thus far and for having blessed the work of the doctor and others who have cared for me.

Give me a humble dependence on Your gracious will, and keep me from becoming impatient, fretful, and distressing to myself and others. Grant me the grace to understand that this illness is Your means to a good end for me. Purify my faith during these days so that I gain a keener sense of values, a better understanding of Your goodness, and a deeper appreciation of the blessings that surround me.

You will not fail me or forsake me. In You I hope day and night. Hear my prayer for Jesus' sake. Amen.

4

Almighty and all-wise Father, I have been sick,

and You are making me well. For Your assistance on the road to recovery I give You humble thanks. I know You can make me completely well if it is Your will. You who commands the sun and the stars can also command my sickness leave. The doctors and nurses are Your instruments; but You bless, and You heal.

I desire so much to be restored to health that I may again perform my duties and participate in the activities I enjoy. I prefer to be helpful to others rather than to have others wait on me. If You will make me well again, I shall praise and glorify You by serving others the rest of my life.

However, if the road to recovery is long and painful, hold me by Your loving hand, so that I may always feel You near me. Make me cheerful, considerate, and appreciative of kindnesses received. Above all, forgive me my sins through the blood of Jesus Christ, and make me holy in Your sight. Give me that peace which the world cannot give. And when I reach journey's end, take me with You to heaven, where there is fullness of joy and where pain and sorrow are no more. Grant these requests for Jesus' sake. Amen.

5

During these days of recovery, gracious Lord, keep me calm and relaxed, unworried and untroubled. Let me always be mindful of Your love, for You are the eternal Caretaker of the souls of all people and are also thinking of me. In Your wisdom and goodness direct my life that I may know each hour You are mindful of my welfare. I thank You and praise Your precious name day after day. Let Your healing hand speed my recovery, and help me to wait patiently on You without complaint. Bless those who take care of me. Grant that they perform their tasks cheerfully. Watch over all the sick, and draw them nearer with Your healing grace through Jesus Christ, my Friend and Savior. Amen.

At the Approach of Death

Lord Jesus Christ, Good Shepherd, I pray You to be with me in the hour of death. Let me feel even now the comfort and the assurance of Your presence. Give me the faith to say: "Even though I walk through the valley of the shadow of death, I fear no evil, for Thou art with me; Thy rod and Thy staff, they comfort me."

Comfort me with the assurance that You have redeemed me from all sin, from death, and from the power of the devil and that I am Yours whether I live or die.

Enable me in the face of death firmly to believe that Your glorious resurrection from the dead has brought life and immortality to light. Give me the blessed hope that in You all shall be made alive, and that I, too shall live again. "O Death, where is thy victory? O Death, where is thy sting? . . . Thanks be to God, who gives us the victory through our Lord Jesus Christ."

May Your Holy Spirit preserve me in this faith until I reach the heavenly land. Amen, Lord Jesus, Amen.

After a Death in the Family

Heavenly Father, the death of my dear _____ has filled my eyes with tears and my heart with sorrow. I am distressed by the mysteries of Your providence. As Your child I want so much to say, "Not my will, but Thine be done," but at times I find it difficult to do. Forgive me and help me, I pray You, by Your Holy Spirit, to accept Your ways as always best.

Apply to my wounded heart the healing touch of Your precious promises, and let me soon experience its power. Teach me not to mourn as those who have no hope. Wipe away the tears from my eyes that I may be able to see through the mist, beyond death and grave, to the resurrection and life assured by the glorious victory of my Savior Jesus Christ over death and grave.

May the passing of my _____ remind me that I, too, am but a pilgrim and stranger on earth.

Grant me the grace to love less and less the things that are material and temporal, and to love more and more the things that are spiritual and eternal. Teach me to number my days and to apply my heart to the wisdom taught by Jesus Christ, that He is the Way and the Truth and the Life, and that no one comes to You but by Him. Amen.

For the Sorrowing

O Father of mercies and God of all comfort, look down upon me in my sorrow and affliction. Comfort me with Your gracious consolations. As an earthly father pities his children, have compassion on me in my suffering. May the loss I have suffered be for me a token of Your love. In my distress lift me up to You. Remind me that in Your mysterious providence all things work together for good to them that love You. You have ordained that I together with all believers must through much tribulation enter into Your kingdom.

May the fiery furnace of affliction, into which You have cast me, by the mercies of Christ refine my heart from the filth of sin and help me to emerge a stronger Christian, better equipped to understand the problems and to deal with the troubles of others. Cause the loss that I have suffered to remind me that the things of earth are like a shadow that does not continue, that I may be inclined to set my affections on things above and not on things on earth. But above all, grant me the sure conviction that Your will and Your ways are best; through Jesus Christ, our Lord. Amen.

Intercessions for the Sick

1

O God of mercy and of might, with whom nothing is impossible, and whose delight is to come to aid of the afflicted and distressed, show Yourself the very present Help in the sickness which has befallen _____ . Comfort him (her) with the blessed assurance of the forgiveness of his (her) sins and grant him (her) patience in suffering until in Your wisdom and gracious providence he (she) may be restored to health again, that the glory of his (her) restoration may be Yours and we all may praise and magnify Your power and love, through Jesus Christ, our Savior. Amen.

2

Almighty and most merciful God, You are the great Physician, and we come before You with a prayer in behalf of _____ , who lies in dire need of help. You know the pain, the danger, and the temptations that have beset him (her), and You alone can provide the relief and help that will perfectly answer the needs that here present themselves. We ask You with full confidence in Your love and power that You may graciously behold, visit, and relieve Your distressed child and grant him (her) the joy of praising You for his (her) deliverance. Teach us all to value health and strength as a precious gift from You and help us to join in thanksgiving for all the healing You daily provide in our bodies and souls, through Jesus Christ, our Lord. Amen.

3

Almighty, everlasting God, the eternal Salvation of them that believe, hear our prayers in behalf of Your servants who are sick, for whom we implore the aid of Your mercy. Graciously heal their bodies and refresh their souls with Your comfort, that, being restored to health, they may give thanks to You in Your church; through Jesus Christ, Your Son, our Lord. Amen.

Table Prayers

Grace at Meals

1

At this table be our Host,
Father, Son, and Holy Ghost!
Food and drink are from above,
Tokens of Your heavenly love.
Amen.

2

Lord God, our heavenly Father, bless this food
that You have given. Cause it to nourish my body
that I may be able to better serve You and those
about me; for Jesus' sake. Amen.

3

Heavenly Father, with sincere appreciation we
accept these gifts coming from Your bountiful hand
and gracious heart. Grant that we remain grateful
at all times for Your benedictions and blessings, for
Jesus' sake. Amen.

Lord, You are the Giver of all that is good. We
thank You for the bountiful meal which is spread
before us. We acknowledge this food as a gift of
Your love and as an invitation to bring our needs
and our thanks to You. Bless the food that You
have given. Grant us the grace to receive it as an
undeserved blessing from You, and nourish our
bodies thereby, that we may be able to serve You
more; in the name of Jesus. Amen.

5

We ask You, Lord Jesus, to honor us with Your
presence at our meal. You have graciously provided
the food we are about to eat and have given us the
health to enjoy Your blessings. Sanctify our hearts
to receive Your blessings to our profit and to Your
great joy. Amen.

Prayers of Thanks

1

Heavenly Father,
  For these blessings from Your store
  Keep me thankful evermore. Amen.

2

Dear Father in heaven, we thank You for the

food we eat. We thank You for the friends we meet. We thank You for Your loving care. In Jesus' name we thank You. Amen.

3

We give thanks to You, gracious Father in Christ Jesus, for the food that You have provided for us in Your goodness and love. Grant that at all times we recognize Your lovingkindness toward us and show our sincere appreciation of all that we have received. We say thanks in Jesus' name. Amen.

4

Dear Father in heaven, we thank You for the refreshment of body and mind that has come to us through the food that You have given. Make us ever thankful for all gifts of Your mercy, and make us faithful in their use. Show us how best to serve You, and give us the willingness to spend our lives in thankful service to You; in the name of Jesus. Amen.

5

We thank You, Lord God, heavenly Father, for Your faithful providence which we have enjoyed and for Your gracious provision of fellowship with one another and with You. Teach us to receive Your gifts with thanksgiving, that with grateful hearts we may enjoy the gifts that have come from You, who together with the Son and the Holy Ghost are one God and one Lord. Amen.

The Benedictions of the Lord

The Old Testament Benediction

The Lord bless you and keep you: The Lord make His face to shine upon you and be gracious to you; The Lord lift up His countenance upon you and give you peace. Numbers 6:24-26.

The New Testament Benedictions

The grace of the Lord Jesus Christ and the love of God and the fellowship of the Holy Spirit be with you all. 2 Corinthians 13:14.

Now to Him who is able to strengthen you according to my Gospel and the preaching of Jesus Christ, according to the revelation of the mystery which was kept secret for long ages but is now disclosed and through the prophetic writings is made known to all nations, according to the command of the eternal God, to bring about the obedience of faith—to the only wise God be glory for evermore through Jesus Christ! Romans 16:25-27.

Peace be to the brethren, and love with faith, from God the Father and the Lord Jesus Christ.

Grace be with all who love our Lord Jesus Christ with love undying. Ephesians 6:23-24.

Now may the Lord of peace Himself give you peace at all times and in all ways. The Lord be with you all. The grace of our Lord Jesus Christ be with you all. 2 Thessalonians 3:16-18.

The Lord be with your spirit. Grace be with you. 2 Timothy 4:22.

Now may the God of peace who brought again from the dead our Lord Jesus, the Great Shepherd of the sheep, by the blood of the eternal covenant, equip you with everything good that you may do His will, working in you that which is pleasing in His sight, through Jesus Christ, to whom be glory forever and ever. Hebrews 13:20-21.

Grow in grace and in the knowledge of our Lord and Savior Jesus Christ. To Him be the glory both now and to the day of eternity. 2 Peter 3:18.

Now to Him who is able to keep you from falling and to present you without blemish before the presence of His glory with rejoicing, to the only God, our Savior through Jesus Christ our Lord, be glory, majesty, dominion, and authority, before all time and now and for ever. Amen. Jude 24-25.

May the God of hope fill you with all joy and peace in believing, so that by the power of the Holy Spirit you may abound in hope. Romans 15:13.

Now to Him who by the power at work within us is able to do far more abundantly than all that we ask or think to Him be glory in the church and in Christ Jesus to all generations, for ever and ever. Ephesians 3:20-21.

To the King of ages, immortal, invisible, the only God, be honor and glory for ever and ever. 1 Timothy 1:17.

The God of all grace, who has called you to his eternal glory in Christ, will himself restore, establish, and strengthen you. To Him be the dominion for ever and ever. 1 Peter 5:10-11.

Blessing and glory and wisdom and thanksgiving and honor and power and might be to our God for ever and ever. Revelation 7:12.

WHERE TO FIND IT IN THE BIBLE

The Ten Commandments—
    Exodus 20 and Deuteronomy 5

The Lord's Prayer—Matthew 6 and Luke 11

The Beatitudes—Matthew 5

The Parable of the Good Samaritan—Luke 10

The Parable of the Prodigal Son—Luke 15

The Seven Letters of Jesus—Revelation 2 and 3

The Sermon on the Mount—Matthew 5—7

The Seven Words from the Cross—
    Matthew 27; Luke 23; John 19

The Pentecost Account—Acts 2

The Fruits of the Spirit—Galatians 5:22-26

The Penitential Psalms—
  Psalms 6; 32; 38; 51; 102; 130; 143

The Psalm of Moses—Psalm 90

The Lord's Supper—
    Matthew 26; Mark 14; Luke 22; 1 Corinthians 11

The Institution of Baptism—Matthew 28:19, 20

The Sum Total of the Gospel—John 3:16

Salvation Through the Blood of Christ—
    Romans 3:20-28

Tables of Duties: For Children, Ephesians 6:1-3; for Fathers,
    Ephesians 6:4; for Husbands, Ephesians 5:25-33; for Wives,
    Ephesians 5:22-24; for Employers, Ephesians 6:9; for
    Employees, Ephesians 6:5-8; for Citizens, Romans 13 and
    1 Peter 2:13-17.

OUTSTANDING STORIES IN THE BIBLE

The Life of Abraham—Genesis 12—25:10
The Story of Jacob and Rachel—Genesis 29
The Life of Joseph—Genesis 37—50
The Birth and Call of Moses—Exodus 2 and 3
The Story of Balaam and Balak—Numbers 22—24
The Fall of Jericho—Joshua 6
The Conquests of Gideon—Judges 6—8
The Strange Ways of Samson—Judges 13—16
The Story of Ruth—The Book of Ruth
David, the Shepherd Boy—1 Samuel 16 and 17
The Friendship of David and Jonathan—1 Samuel 18 to 20
Elijah the Tishbite—1 Kings 17—21 and 2 Kings 2
The Cleansing of Naaman, the Leper—2 Kings 5
Queen Esther—The Book of Esther
Daniel and His Friends—Daniel 1—6
King Hezekiah—Isaiah 36—39
Jonah and the Great Fish—The Book of Jonah
Job and His Misfortunes—Job 1, 2, 42
The Life of Jesus According to Luke
The Man Born Blind—John 9
The Footwashing in the Upper Room—John 13
Peter and John at the Gate Beautiful—Acts 3
The Shipwreck of Paul—Acts 27 and 28

OUTSTANDING CHAPTERS OF THE OLD TESTAMENT

Genesis 1	2 Chronicles 6
Numbers 35	Job 14
Deuteronomy 28	Job 19
Joshua 1	Job 38
1 Samuel 3	Proverbs 30
2 Samuel 12	Proverbs 31
2 Kings 7	Isaiah 6

Isaiah 40	Ezekiel 37
Isaiah 44	Ezekiel 47
Isaiah 53	Joel 2
Isaiah 61	Malachi 3
Ezekiel 3	

Favorite Psalms

Psalms 2; 19; 23; 24; 27; 37; 42; 46; 51; 63; 84; 90; 91; 100; 103; 118; 121; 139

OUTSTANDING CHAPTERS OF THE NEW TESTAMENT

Matthew 11	Acts 8
Matthew 13	Acts 10
Mark 10	Acts 26
Luke 2	Romans 5
Luke 7	Romans 8
Luke 15	1 Corinthians 13
Luke 16	1 Corinthians 15
Luke 18	Galatians 6
Luke 24	Ephesians 2
John 3	Ephesians 5
John 4	Philippians 4
John 10	Hebrews 11
John 11	James 3
John 14	1 Peter 1
John 15	Revelation 3